Founded in 1964 by John

Voices: *Journal of the Ame*

VOICES: THE ART AND SCIENCE OF PSYCHOTHERAPY (ISSN 0042-8272) is published by the American Academy of Psychotherapists, 230 Washington Ave Ext , Suite 101 / Albany, NY 12203.

Subscription prices for one year (three issues): $65 for individuals PDF only; $85 for individuals PDF & print copy; $249 for institutions. Orders by mail payable by check: 230 Washington Ave Ext, Suite 101 / Albany, NY 12203. Orders by MasterCard or Visa: call (518) 240-1178 or fax (518) 463-8656. Payments must be made in U.S. dollars through a U.S. bank made payable to *AAP Voices.* Some back volumes may be available from the *Voices* Business Office.

Change of Address: Please inform publisher as soon as a change to your email address is made. Send change of email address to aap@caphill.com.

Journal of The American Academy of Psychotherapists

VOICES

THE ART AND SCIENCE OF PSYCHOTHERAPY

If winter enshrouds the soul in a chrysalis, then spring sees its reemergence. If we've used the quiet, solitary days of winter well, we approach spring with a soul that has had its inner resources tested and strengthened. We exit the cold stillness and pick up the threads of a busy, active life with fortitude and joy.

—G. Schmidt & S. Felch, eds., *Spring: A Spiritual Biography of the Season*

Journal of the American Academy of Psychotherapists

VOICES

THE ART AND SCIENCE OF PSYCHOTHERAPY

Hope and Rebirth Spring 2022: Volume 58, Number 1

Cover:

Variant #5 Hope by Tom Schulz
https://www.tomschulzartist.com

Published three times per year.
Cover Design: Mary de Wit
Design and Production by
Mary de Wit | in2Wit®, llc
AAP Web Site:
www.aapweb.com

Carla Bauer

Carla R. Bauer, lcsw, is in private practice in Atlanta, Georgia. A second career therapist, she brings over 25 years of corporate experience, as well as an earlier journey in theological studies, to her understanding of people and their struggles. Psychoanalytically trained, she seeks to blend psychodynamic and attachment orientations with a contemporary relational presence. When she can't be on the beach, the colors of the beach are on her! As editor of *Voices*, she offers her voice to AAP.
crbauer01@bellsouth.net

Behold! From Darkness Follows Light

Our theme, *Hope and Rebirth,* explores what sustains us through dark times and how we see or await the return of the light. Envisioning this theme, I thought of how the timing of the issue spanned two seasons of hope and rebirth: We would write during the winter, both a stint of darkness and containing the holiday season of hope and joy, to publish in spring, nature's time of rebirth. Themes of hope and rebirth are reflected in the multiple religions that celebrate these seasons as well as in nature's return of the light after the winter solstice and season of growth and fertility in spring. Just as winter holds both darkness and the hopeful holiday season and celebration of the return of the light, so we wrote while standing hopefully in the waning of pandemic darkness, looking toward the return of light in our lives.

We are tired! Therapists and clients alike—exhausted by isolation, adaptations to telehealth, relentless political and racial unrest, and especially by the prolonged uncertainty of when we will finally escape this pandemic holding pattern and breathe freely again. Clients and therapists alike have reported increased struggles with anxiety and depression, sometimes fear and despair, as pandemic darkness has lingered on, from variant to variant. We are eager to look beyond the heaviness that has weighed us down for too long. We begin to turn now toward the light, seeking hope, joy, rejuvenation, and restoration.

For this issue of *Voices*, authors were invited to consider, in pandemic and other times of darkness, where they find hope of the return of the light. Readers are invited to join with them in pondering: From what do you draw strength? What restores your energy or renews your spirit? Did what brought sustenance in the past hold up against pandemic distress, or did you have to find it in new ways? How have you seen hope and rebirth in your consultation rooms? What keeps hope alive—for you, for your clients, for the world?

I realized early in the pandemic that I could live this time of prolonged isolation as one of darkness or embrace it as one of reset (my version of rebirth). While I can't say that it hasn't held moments of darkness (no one has ever called me Pollyanna), I have written previously of the intentionality with which I have tried to lean in and grasp the unprecedented opportunity for a much-needed reset. And even if that weren't so needed, how could I hope to encourage my clients not to merely languish or mark time but to fully live, albeit differently, this surreal experience, unless I practiced this myself? From that mindset, our theme was uppermost as I entered my second pandemic holiday season, even more intentional than in the first about creating my own celebrations in absence of social gatherings and family traditions.

The holidays have long been a difficult time for me as traditional religious meanings lost their hold and family configurations and celebrations changed. So I was overdue for a holiday refresh. Even if I did nothing more exciting than take those last 2 weeks of the year off from my practice and curl up with a stack of books, alternating with a soft pillow, I was more than ready to lean into that break! But I wanted that and more. I wanted meaningful holidays as well as rest, rejuvenation of soul as well as body. So I decked the halls, queued up the holiday music, sacred and secular, and brought in assorted seasonal treats. When a friend later said of the holidays, "At least we weren't sick" (as so many were, with variants surging), it did not resonate: I didn't want an "at least" stance of surviving dark holidays (or a dark pandemic)—I wanted to lean in and embrace the season of light and hope in the same spirit with which I have tried to lean into the whole of pandemic time.

Inspired by a 2020 Hallmark holiday movie, *Love, Lights, Hanukkah!*, in which a young woman, raised Catholic by an adoptive mother, learns of her biological Jewish heritage just in time to celebrate Hanukkah with a newly found birth family, I decided to honor my own dotted-line heritage (as I imagine it might be depicted on a genogram) in celebrating the 2021 holidays. My father was adopted by a Jewish man and Christian woman, she a relative of his biological mother. My grandfather did not live his Jewish heritage, so my father was not raised in any identification with it, and neither in turn was I. But though it is neither my bloodline nor familial culture, a significant early life attachment to my great-uncle (that grandfather's brother) has left me with a soul affinity to Judaism that he himself may not have had. I remember a long-ago schoolyard debate between friends of different Christian denominations over the appropriate age for baptism and the implications for heaven if one died before receiving this sacrament. I recall declaring, "If Major (my uncle) won't be in heaven, I don't want to go there either."

I don't actually remember Major—he died when I was only 3—but I grew up on such rich stories of his particular devotion to me that I have felt his loss for as long as I can remember. I did not have the language of attachment back then that I have now for understanding the impact of this early relationship, but I knew it had been profound even if only "remembered" second-hand via the stories. Looking at pictures now, seeing his keen attunement to my every toddler whim, I can almost feel the bewilderment that I must have felt when suddenly he was gone. A light had surely gone out in my world! Borrowing again from psychotherapy language I didn't have then, I have an internal

3-year-old part that still wanders about wondering where Major went. She and I have spent much pandemic time together, holding close our attachments from other times in their now ever-present absence. I don't have the same assumptions today about any afterlife reunion in the heaven of that young baptism debate—I can only stay open to the unknown—but I know as surely now as I knew in that schoolyard that if it were not to include Major (or the many Jewish friends who now people my life) because of a difference in faith...well then, it need not include me either. What would be the point?

So, fast forward many years, I decided to light the Hanukkah menorah in honor of this attachment heritage and as a holding of hope amidst all that darkened our world at the time of this holiday season (and still): even the pandemic seeming to take a backseat to the racial, political, and climate turmoil that threatened (threatens) our country and the world beyond. (And that was before the Russian invasion of Ukraine and the threat of nuclear war that hangs darkly over the world today.)

Overlapping the 8 days of that ritual, in a similar holding of hope, I embraced the daily rites of my chocolate Advent calendar (religion might be in question, but my belief in chocolate is absolute!) and Jostein Gaarder's (1996) Advent story, *The Christmas Mystery*, similarly consumed in daily installments. In it, a young boy discovers a magical Advent calendar: Each day, as he opens a new door to behold the hidden picture behind it, a slip of paper falls out, unfolding a mysterious story in which a young girl chases a toy lamb come to life as it runs out of a Norwegian department store. With Joachim, readers follow Elisabet as she pursues the little lamb back through the ages and across the globe, gathering along the way more sheep, shepherds, angels, and the wise kings of Orient, all journeying to Bethlehem for the holy birth. Gaarder breathed new life into an old familiar story and into my holiday observance.

Perhaps as powerful as any deeper religious meaning might be, the daily ritual of these practices held space for hope, mindfulness, and intentionality, much as new pandemic era morning routines of coffee on the deck and second-cup poetry reading have done throughout the year. These practices of grounding self before meeting the demands of the day have been a big part of holding light amidst pandemic darkness and allowing space for change and reset. I can only hope that however their forms might vary when (someday) post-pandemic life resumes, something of these daily rites will stick. It is increasingly clear that this pandemic does not end with a return to normal. The life I had pre-pandemic is in many respects gone; reemergence will be a starting anew, building on both what was there before and what was born of pandemic life.

New rites and rituals continue. I write this having just attended my first Passover Seder, which again turns my thoughts to the movement from darkness into light—from slavery and oppression to freedom and liberation. In addition to recounting the story of Exodus, the Passover Haggadah held memory of the Holocaust and space for slaveries and oppressions of any form. It was a natural fit to weave in readings about the war in Ukraine—a holding of both hope and unity amidst this current darkness of oppression. We can express in war, as in pandemic or any dark time, the hope that there will be a later, a time in which things will be different, better. Surviving comes through holding space for light, holding hope for possibility. We know this well; we convey it in our consultation rooms all the time to inject hope and ward off despair when clients are catastrophizing from the place where all they can see is their current darkness lasting forever. Now, watching what and how the Ukrainians endure, day after day, week upon week, we have a new model for resilience.

Rounding out observance of the spring rites of rebirth, my inner 3-year-old and I dyed Easter eggs together. I haven't done that since I wasn't much older than 3! Leaning in to the seasons and the moment—even a pandemic—draws light out of darkness.

In this issue, authors offer their reflections on hope and resilience in times of darkness. Many of our authors found resilience a more graspable concept than hope at this time. Zoe Worrell and Grover Criswell each exegete the meanings of the word "hope" and what it offers us. Carole Light explores her resistance to the concept of hope but perhaps finds it in staying present to what is and to possibility, and Judy Lazarus shares her own story of finding hope amidst tragedy in the possibility of change. Avrum Weiss voices the hope of emerging from isolation and reconnecting.

Rhona Engles presents a photo essay evoking the powerful solace of nature, in pandemic and other times; she tries to hold hope that this solace won't soon be darkened by our refusal to heed the perils of climate change. Jonathan Farber shows how hope can be found in unexpected places, positing to the skeptic (in himself and others) that embracing it can't hurt and just might help. Linda Tillman, too, finds hope rising from an unexpected place, and *Voices* graphic designer, Mary de Wit, illustrates her own hopeful take on a popular pandemic pastime. Susan Berlin shares her story of personal transformation during the pandemic, while Kristie Nies's account of physical resilience and recovery demonstrates hope manifested in deliberate action. John Rhead puts his hope in psychotherapy to help bring healing to the world.

In a special feature, authors explore the theme of drawing resilience from pets, as so many have particularly done amidst pandemic isolation. Kay Loveland provides context for the role of pets in therapy and resiliency work and shares her own story of the role of the person-pet connection during an extended illness. Don Murphy captures the light a new dog brought into pandemic darkness. Annie Prescott narrates how the rhythm of life in her pet menagerie contributed to her recovery from a major surgery. Barbara Sachs, Stephanie Ezust, and Giuliana Reed each pay tribute to beloved pets lost during the pandemic. And Bradley Lake shares his story of how two dogs brought their human partners together to build a family.

Neal Whitman, J Grant, Joanna Frederick, and Tom Large share original poems reflecting themes of hope and resilience. Giuliana Reed's watercolor painting, *New Day*, expresses that hope through a creative pandemic pastime. And in book reviews, Stephanie Ezust summarizes lessons learned from Jane Goodall and Douglas Abrams in their timely new book, *The Book of Hope: A Survival Guide for Trying Times.*

Laying out this issue as spring unfolds and daylight lengthens, we move about a bit more freely and feel a tad more hope of a return to something resembling normal times, however changed we and the world might be by our pandemic experience. We begin to reconnect. Our Summer 2022 theme, *Borders and Walls: Facing the Other*, will explore what still divides us.

If you read something that speaks to you, let the authors know. Keep voices connecting! ▼

Zoë Worrell

Zoë Worrell, LCSW-C, is a psychotherapist in Ocean Isle Beach, North Carolina, where she settled in 2021 with her husband of 42 years to start a new life adventure near the sand and sea. She provides therapy to adults and enjoys supervising new clinicians along their path as therapists. Zoë resonates deeply with the Celtic spiral symbol, remaining ever curious about how life unfolds and how the self grows.
Irishzoe14@gmail.com

Hope:
An Often Overused and Misunderstood Word Made Up of Four Letters, One of Which Is Inconspicuously Silent

Hope. What a small, but fascinating word. A noun, a verb, and if you add a few more letters, an adjective or adverb. Depending on what thesaurus you use online, hope has between 100 and 125 synonyms—that's quite an array of words one could use to capture the meaning of this complicated word.

So where do we start to define, comprehend, or otherwise appreciate this term? I'll start with some of the obvious explanations. As a noun, hope implies an anticipation, a longing, or a wish. For example, "I have a hope that these musings are good enough for publication in *Voices*." To have hope is to hold a precious gem of expectation, usually but not necessarily, toward something positive or good. Hope as a noun serves to describe something that rests in the moments to come.

Then we have hope as a verb—and how overused, trite, and at times down right boring a verb it is. Consider how many times you have most likely used this word in casual conversation: "I hope you feel better." "Here's hoping the weather is good for the wedding." Or the ever popular, "Hope all is well with you." (Consider me guilty as charged.) As a verb, hope implies the action of belief, the philosophy of faith, or the notion of trust in the future and its implications.

If we go to the inverse of hope, we arrive at despair, another noun, albeit incredibly more depressing. Although gloomy, despair does help to highlight the upbeat nature of hope. Hope and despair, yin and yang, dark and light, sadness and joy—each counterpart accentuating the meaning of the other and helping us to garner a deeper knowing of both. Within this context, hope is the beacon that shines brightly before us when we're lost in the murky fog. Granted, I would argue that we need to accept the idea of embracing both—but I digress and will get back to the subject at hand.

So other than adding a few more letters to get to an adjective or adverb, how else might we describe hope? In my mind, hope on a dimension beyond a part of speech becomes a thing to encounter, something to sense, a phenomenon to experience. This is where things get complicated. How do I describe my meetings with a felt sense of hope? I'll give it my best effort in the illustrations to follow.

What comes to mind first are those exquisite moments that show up now and then in my role as therapist: 40-year-old Evan, for example. Evan, whose early life was wrought with trauma and grief, showed up weekly and sat across from me expounding on the fact that life has always hurt and would continue to always hurt. His depression and despair sometimes felt irreversible, and I often found myself experiencing a heaviness when I sat with him. Then, weeks, months (it actually might have been years) later, a moment happened that struck out and hit me with, yes you guessed it, the felt sense of hope. What began as the regular melancholy cadence of our sessions suddenly took a sharp turn. I can't now remember the specific words that were conveyed or why they held such pertinence, but something broke open within him, and a salty tear or two cascaded down his face. And there it was within me, something that I can only describe as lovely and warm and bright—a feeling of hope.

Next, I travel to a moment filled with personal sadness and grief. My son-in-law had passed away suddenly in a tragic accident, and my daughter, her two boys, Finn and Liam (ages 3 and 6), my husband, my son, and I were gathered around a tree we had just planted in honor of Patrick's life. In the midst of digging the hole, setting the Colorado Spruce in the empty space, and sharing in the ritual of placing dirt around its tender roots, we heard a repeated screeching noise emanating from the skies above. With tears in our eyes and heavy hearts, we looked upward and witnessed the origin of this piercing sound: a redtail hawk circling overhead, calling us to witness the majesty of all it was. A remarkable raptor, a sizable bird that, serendipitously, Patrick had often pointed out to his boys, was soaring above the fields around us.

And then the moment happened—Liam, all 6 years of his little wounded soul—spoke out loud, "Some people say that when somebody dies, their spirit goes into an animal, and they show up to let us know they are okay." I was emotionally slayed, and in that moment, my grief took on an energy that I can only describe as some kind of soul-light that let me know there was more to life than loss and despair. The felt sense of hope resonated again throughout my being.

I have so many more memories of what I now refer to as the feeling, the awareness, of hope. They have showed up in seemingly simple things—when I'm having a tough day and all 50 pounds of my sweet goldendoodle, Doogan, jumps up and lathers me with kisses, or when many years ago someone anonymously dropped off bags of groceries for our family because my single mother couldn't afford to feed five hungry kids. Even the smallest of moments can evoke the warmth of hope for me—like the time someone ahead of me at Dunkin Donuts paid for my cup of tea and blueberry donut or a driver letting me enter the long line of traffic with a smile and a wave. To be honest, the sunrise, trees blooming in spring, or fresh fallen snow can also illicit a sense of hope in me.

With these reflections, I return to the idea that hope is a complex word, so much deeper than its dictionary meaning or the plethora of words we can find in the thesaurus that are related to it. In my opinion, hope is also a deeply felt experience, one that speaks to a vital facet of our collective humanity. Hope is a moment when I feel larger than the "me" I usually hang out with. Hope is a sense of something more expansive, and maybe more treasurable, than ordinary life moments—a feeling that allows me to connect with all that is human within me.

Perhaps in the end, this felt sense, this awareness, of hope is a subtle nuance of a complicated word made up of four simple letters. It's as if the first three letters of hope are there to shout out how it is defined and thought of, and the silent "e" is the whisper that reminds us to sit still and let the experience of hope softly embrace us. ▼

> Hope is being able to see that there is light despite all of the darkness.
>
> —Desmond Tutu

> Life begins on the other side of despair.
>
> —Sartre

KING

Grover E. Criswell

Grover E. Criswell, MDiv, is a retired psychotherapist whose practice was in Dayton, Ohio. In his professional life he has worn many hats besides therapist: minister, hospital chaplain, social activist, workshop leader both nationally and internationally, and writer, having published over 35 articles, many in *Voices* where he has been on the editorial board for 32 years. He joined the American Academy of Psychotherapists in 1975 and is a past president and fellow. These days he is active in the World House Choir (singing the music of justice and equality), the Dayton Book Guys (a men's book club that has been going for 25 years), and as a First Reader for the Dayton Literary Peace Prize.
grovyale1960@gmail.com

Searching for Hope

We have seen it before, even though not quite like this, that in the immediacy of the moment, the catastrophe is overwhelming. The devastation in Kentucky from the monster tornado that ripped through that state is beyond description: piles of shattered debris, mounds of smashed belongings, the destroyed treasures of a lifetime, flipped cars, block after block annihilated and laid to waste. Looking on this scene from the security of television, we wonder how this community and the people who live there can ever possibly deal with this crushing blow. It is difficult to imagine how they will ever get their lives back on track. When we are honest with ourselves, we are thankful this didn't happen to us because we carry some worry whether we could find the ability to generate hope again. Yet the very next day, standing in the middle of the rumble, the governor of Kentucky not only acknowledged how terrible was the storm but proclaimed a message of hope that they would build back what had been lost. Several of the residents who were interviewed also simultaneously expressed grief and hopefulness, looking ahead with confidence to building anew.

The question this raises is what is this phenomenon called hope? What is it, and how do we get it when in a crisis we need it? The myriad and wobbly definitions of hope don't help. Sometimes hope is loosely defined as wishing, hankering, or craving, the satisfaction of a personalized want or desire. (For example: The child hoped he would get a bike for Christmas. She hoped that she had chosen the winning lottery ticket. He held out hope that he would get the job.) Only a specific outcome is satisfactory. Others see hope as feeding a delusional system clutching to the power of positive thinking, a desperate optimism in the face of harsh reality. Hope gives promise when the only other option is despair. But from where does that hope come? On what is it based? These limited attempts at defining hope do not guide us to clarity or encourage us when facing dark times. We need more.

We live in a world where feeling hopeful is difficult. Climate change is wreaking havoc across the planet, and the blight in Kentucky is only a sample of increasingly scary occurrences. As I am writing this article, the Omicron variant is declining, but we are reminded that it is not going away. Even as mandates are lifted, those not vaccinated are still at great risk. People are still being hospitalized and are dying. What is safe? Not only is the possibility of catching COVID-19 frightening, but the limits it has imposed on social structures and communal interaction are crippling. Then there are the thousands mobilizing to overthrow our democracy and trash what have been significant traditions. They are outlawing books and limiting the right to vote. They seem to be winning. All of these hectic and threatening macro dynamics are in addition, of course, to the personal losses and fearful situations visited upon us uniquely, sometimes without any warning.

My first lessons about hope were from my parents. They were lower middle class, and my mother was often ill, but they were always hopeful about the future. I am sure their religious roots were part of this. In Ponca City, Oklahoma, there is a statue entitled "The Pioneer Woman." She stands tall, wind blowing in her hair, holding one child with two clinging close to her legs, and holds her head high looking to the West with resilience. That statue always reminded me of my mother. My parents modeled for me the belief that no matter what happened, I could deal with it just the way they had. I have certainly had many situations where I have wondered whether that was true, but for the most part that stance has given me an advantage.

Yet where I have learned most about hope over these many years is with my clients. Many who sought me out were struggling with feeling hopeful. They had suffered loss by death or estrangement, defeats and disappointments, insecurity, or fear. What they have taught me is this: In finding the way to hope, you have to acknowledge the reality of the darkness and express the feelings that go with that. There is no quick road to hope that can dodge the pain of loss or the darkness of distress, or bury the vulnerability of fright. There is no quick switch to turn on the light. Too frequently, those trying to help admonish those feeling hopeless to hurry up and get over it. Think positive! The grieving or fearful person then goes silent or slips into depression. Climbing the mountain to hope often means spending enough time with the awful feelings in the desert.

Some years ago I was attending a weekend workshop at the Cleveland Gestalt Institute. Late that night there was a knock on my door, and I thought it was another group participant. Wrong! Two guys with guns held me up and took all of my money. Mostly I was terrified, never having had any similar experience. The only good part was that the group the next day gave me healing support with expressing the terror and trauma of that event. They helped me get back on my feet.

Finding hope means discovering inner strength. Solidity in our sense of self and the gift of personal attributes helps, but the greatest lessons come from the memory of dealing with difficult circumstances, those times when we fell down and lifted ourselves back up. Often in the middle of a crisis we forget who we are and the abilities we possess. Only as we are grounded in the present can we see much possibility for the future. This is frequently the work of therapy: kindling anew the promise of hope by looking inside. Once I had a tenured professor as a client who felt totally defeated by the university system of which he was a part. He didn't like the courses he was expected to teach year after year and felt that none of his colleagues shared his interests. He felt himself in an isolated hole with no relief. Needless to say, he didn't feel very hopeful about the future. In therapy, exploring his feelings about all of this, he began to feel again some of his old identity. He devised a course of his own, worked to finish a book he had started, and used the Internet to find other professors who shared his interests. He became more confident about his future, and his energy returned.

What was also evident at the destruction in Kentucky was the vast number of people who immediately gathered to give help. They came from miles around and were eager to search for survivors, clean up the debris, and begin the process of rebuilding. They functioned as a community without political or religious differences. Their very presence gave encouragement. When bad things happen, the support of others aids in dealing with the trauma and believing in the future. Our family and friends enable us to move forward. Hope is always enhanced by communal support. Time and again I have seen this as the fruit of the therapeutic relationship, especially in group psychotherapy.

Finally, the hope that sustains us is an existential commitment toward the future. This choice in the direction of possibility can frequently have an influence on what evolves. I have often found helpful the admonition of the perceptual psychologist George Kelly (1963): "A person's processes are psychologically channelized by the ways in which he anticipates events" (p. 46). Being hopeful does not mean that we can predict what the future holds or that it will be exactly what we want. We certainly get no guarantees the future will always be happy and joyful. Hope is banking on our ability to deal with what comes. In the dark times, even standing in the rumble with intense feelings, yet remembering who we are and surrounded by those who support us, we stay hopeful to what the future might bring. ▼

References

Kelly, G. (1963). *A theory of personality: The psychology of personal constructs.* New York: WW Norton and Company.

Carole Light, PhD

Scaly Mountain,
North Carolina
carolelight@hotmail.com

Hope

I never much liked the concept of hope. As I thought about writing for this *Voices* issue on "Hope and Rebirth," I began to focus with more curiosity on what it is that I attach to hope that makes it feel unappealing. I came up with an immediate association on the other side of hope, which is disappointment, hope unrealized. To me, hope feels passive, silent, and isolated. More comfortable, as I sit with this, are concepts like curiosity, staying in the present, patience, trusting in the inevitability of change, finding the power to take some action even if that action is just to change my thoughts, my projections on the future. A bit of Buddhist influence, I suspect.

Jane Goodall, with Douglas Abrams, has written a book published in 2021 called *The Book of Hope: A Survival Guide for Trying Times*. She suggests that taking action and having hope are circular. You have to have hope that taking action can lead to change or you become passive. So, she says, hope is circular, generated by action. It is when, for one reason or another, I have been unable to take action that I have also not been able to connect with hope. I believe that is the case with many clients struggling with depression.

An alternative to hope, which is really future-focused, is to allow oneself to stay fully in the present. Of course, in grief, depression, or terminal illness the experience of your present may feel frightening to embrace. Rather than hope, I encourage myself and others to trust that what is the present experience will not stay the same. Everything is constantly changing. There is no promise the change will seem better; it might seem worse, but that, too, will change if one just stays with the thoughts, feelings, and fears. Memories of other situations may pop up, thoughts of people not presently available, and allowing oneself to be fully engaged with what comes up will alter the mood or feeling, if only for a moment. And that moment can matter a lot if noticed.

One powerful memory from my own deep personal work illustrates this experience and has shaped my beliefs. Just after I was divorced, with a 3-year-old child, I was scared, overwhelmed, felt totally alone with this gigantic life task of raising a little boy. The powerful work I did, guided by an Academy colleague, impacted my experience of despair and hope for the rest of my life. I was encouraged to close my eyes and fully feel the fear, loneliness, and despair that I was describing. I was guided to attend to the feelings in my body and simply allow them to be there while at the same time invite an image of the experience to form. For what seemed like a very long time, my image was simply darkness. Nothing happened. Slowly, I began to see myself with my son in a vast ocean, floating in a small rubber boat, being tossed and rocked by the sea. The instructions were, "Just stay with it, and see what happens next." So I did, for what seemed like another very long time. And then, to my surprise, I saw a huge whale swimming nearby, and I felt protected and less alone. I stayed with that image for a while and then, to my delight, I saw a distant shore line and felt the whale gently guiding me to shore. After a soft landing I had the awareness of people living nearby and felt the possibility of unexpected help from sources not yet known. I guess that could be called "hope," or, more to my liking, staying in the presence of what is, allowing it to change, opening to unknown possibilities.

When I indulge in hope, I think I try to be more specific about what I am hoping for. Knowing it will inevitably change, I experience more openness to mystery, having less control, allowing, and living in to the new possibility. Perhaps, in the end, it is just semantics. ▼

References

Goodall, J. & Abrams, D. (2021). *The book of hope: A survival guide for trying times.* New York: Celadon Books.

Survival is to imagine hope even when we cannot see it or feel it. It is a practice like any other. The more we do it the more we can call on it in times of need.

—Kathryn Van der Heiden

Nescitur Ignescitur – Unknown It Burns

an ekphrastic response to *Pandora* painted by Dante Gabriel Rossetti in 1871

Neal Whitman

Behold! A portrait! Pandora!
Her brightly lit oval face and neck
the color of ivory is framed
by dark, cascading chestnut hair.
Her blue eyes stare straight at us.
Does she see us ... or perhaps
the misfortunes that are yet to come?
Pandora is cradling a box that forever
will carry her name – derived
from *pan* (all) *doran* (gift). Such gifts!

Her right hand, also brightly lit,
atop her eponymous box;
her left hand under it. Her fingers
clenched, hold the box shut tight.
Her red lips also shut tight. Her body
from the thigh up and the background
are all in dark palette, as if
she disappears in the mists of time.
We see the last wisps of smoke
still seeping from the box.

Such gifts! She had been warned
not to open the box ... but Pandora was
formed by the Gods with a shameless mind.
She let loose into the world,
"hard toil along with ills and heavy sickness." *
We detect on Pandora's countenance
regret, but perhaps not remorse.
Could she have known that, when
in panic she shut the lid, trapped
inside was *Elpis*, Goddess of Hope?

Elpis! Sounds like Help Us, eh?
Hope is the antidote for despair.
We count on Hope to carry on
during difficult times. But, if Hope
remains at the bottom of the box,
how can we render troubles
and sorrows less painful in life?
Alas, look again at the painting –
on the box this dire warning:
Nescitur Ignescitur – Unknown It Burns.

Descry the swirling smoke.
Does it foreshadow and portend
inconsolable grief and lament?
Rossetti put on paper a poem
what his oils had applied to canvas.
His sonnet opens, *What of the end?*
   And closes thus,
Thou mayst not dare to think; nor canst thou
      know
   If Hope still pent there be dead or alive.

Is Hope a gift that comes to us,
divine largesse, or must we be
worthy of its endowment, or
do we have to make it happen?
Is it up to The Gods or up to us
to find Hope in imagination and courage?
Some day will Covid drift away
and disappear like smoke, or will
its dark cloud hover over us with no end?
Who will release *Elpis* and bring us Hope?

* ancient Greek poet, Hesiod, *Work and Days*

靈寶始青變化之圖

Judy Lazarus

The Map of Change:
Holding Hope in the Face of Harsh Reality

Judy Lazarus, LCSW-C, earned her master's degree in social work from The Catholic University of America in 1972. During her nearly 50 years of practice, she has worked with children, adolescents, and families. Her own family of five children served as deep teachers of the complex joys of staying open for the surprise. She lives in Edgewater, Maryland.
liuloo@aol.com

> *Hope is miles removed from both pessimism and optimism. Hope deals with reality. And reality is surprising. ... Hope is openness for that surprise. ...hope is not the conviction that everything will turn out fine. That's optimism. Hope thrives in the midst of hopelessness. Hopelessness is not the opposite of hope. Despair is the opposite of hope. In the midst of hopelessness, hope thrives because it will not give into despair. Although the situation is hopeless, there is always room for surprise. Hope says, 'Let's stay open for the surprise.' Not the surprise of a happy ending, Hollywood style. That's mere optimism and it is proved unrealistic at every turn. But to remain open for the surprise when everything turns out much worse than we could ever imagine—that is hope. Despair assigns reality a deadline. Hope knows that there are no deadlines for reality.*
>
> —*David Steindl-Rast (1987)*

How to stay open for the surprise after life events have walloped you a few times has been the focus of myriad psychotherapy sessions over the years. The above quote and the longer article in which it originated have guided me through many such struggles to hold hope, stay open to surprise, in the face of harsh life experiences, rather than give in to false deadlines for reality's final act.

The Ancient Chinese Map of Change that hangs in my office reminds me to hold this openness for hope. The map came into my awareness in 1984. At the time, I was a happily married 39-year-old mother of three sons, working in solo practice 2 long days a week. I loved the rhythm and push of my life and felt grateful for the space to raise my kids and work at something meaningful.

My friend Walter was like a fostering sort of "uncle" who took me under his wing when I first moved from the flatlands of Ohio to Washington, DC, in 1970. I lived for a few years in the efficiency apartment building he managed. We became friends, and he helped me integrate into the culture of his salon. Most of us residents of the building were just starting out in life. Walter made sure we socialized and looked out for each other through our Friday drinks and snacks at his apartment.

A widower with one son who lived in Colorado, Walter was an enchanting, classically educated man in his 70s. After graduating from Williams College, he joined a group of teachers who travelled to China for missionary work. Later, he taught Latin and Greek to high school students in Massachusetts. During World War II he enlisted and served in the South Pacific, where he survived the Bataan Death March. Back home, he married his long-time sweetheart, and they raised their son in Colorado, where they were both teachers. After her death, Walter moved to Washington where he intended to retire in the Old Soldiers Home, only to find the company of his fellow retirees too tame. He moved out and took a job managing an apartment house around Dupont Circle, working part time teaching in DC public schools and hauling bales of Washington Post newspapers off the back of a truck delivering to newsstands on the weekends. Somehow, he was a member of the Harvard Business Club and took various women who resided at the apartment house to fancy lunchtime lectures each month. Walter led a very busy life and changed my ideas about how older people could entertain themselves. He was a crusty old survivor. With his perpetual stogie and Ivy League restraint, he knew how to play and enjoyed a great range of experience.

Walter was my first real emotional connection in DC. I could trust him. He had become an unexpected friend and confidant. Even after I left his nest, we maintained a dear friendship. When Walter called to let me know he had cancer, he invited us to meet his son, John, who had moved to the area to live near his father while he lived out his last months.

I was trying to figure out my grief when I found *The Tao of Physics*, by Fritjof Capra (1975). It seemed like the kind of dense book about science that would give me answers about how I could bear to let him go. Every night, after putting the kids to bed, I read some pages before sleeping so I could change channels from everyday life. I was flummoxed by Schrödinger's cat. I learned about light moving as a wave or a particle in the eye of the beholder. These stories made me more hopeful somehow about Walter not being in this world anymore.

One night, I turned the page and found the Ancient Chinese Map of Change. The conceit that one could draw the process of change initially made me laugh. But my eyes became intent on following the way the energy flowed—light against dark. I found it tremendously soothing. I found myself going back to look at it again and again—imagining where I was on the road of light into dark. Some days it felt like I was on the straightaway; other days I was looping. Having this map for daily spiritual navigation/meditation helped me cope.

I kept reading and visiting Walter at hospice that summer, preparing myself for his death. Then, in mid-August, my youngest son, Devin, drowned in a backyard swimming pool accident. Our family was devastated. My world came apart. Walter and his son came to the funeral and held me and mine in our desolation. Months later, we held John after Walter died. John copied the Ancient Chinese Map of Change as a remembrance. It still helps me cope.

In the last 2 years, I have Zoomed from my office with the Ancient Chinese Map of Change in the background of my vision—all the dark and light of my clients' lives and my own life satisfyingly caught in its small frame. It helps me stay open to changes in my world that are confounding and that I hate in the moment. It helps me hold space for surprise around the next turn, to hold hope. All is well—I have the map! ▼

References

Capra, F. (1975). *The Tao of physics: An exploration of the parallels between modern physics and Eastern mysticism.* Boulder, CO: Shambhala Publications.

Steindl-Rast, D. (1987). The shadow. *The Sun,* 137, April 1987, 20-23.

> Something that is mysterious for one second is often quenched like an empty oil lamp in the next. Yet, if only we turn our heads in another direction, a new light may be lighted there.
>
> —Jostein Gaarder

> All shall be well, and all shall be well, and all manner of things shall be well.
>
> —St. Julian of Norwich

Avrum Weiss, PhD

Vinalhaven, Maine
agweiss@comcast.net

Isolation

A Personal Perspective: Our adaptability is a blessing and a curse.

People say we've got it made
Don't they know we're so afraid?
Isolation

—John Lennon

English zoologist Desmond Morris (1969) suggested that human beings rose to their position of dominance on the planet because we were more adaptable than other creatures. Humans learned a variety of skills that allowed us to gather food from a wide range of environments, whereas other creatures went hungry when the food in their limited environments became scarce. Being adaptable is both a blessing and a curse, though. Adaptability gives us the flexibility to survive challenging circumstances, but the downside is our tendency to adapt so well that we don't notice how bad things really are. There is an urban myth that if you put a frog in a pot of cold water and very slowly bring the water to a boil the frog will never notice the incremental changes in differences until it has boiled to death. So it is with COVID.

I went for a walk with my dog this morning, as we do every morning. It's not our usual day to go to the bakery, but we went to see Stephanie and chatted about her husband Tom who is in the beginning stages of cancer treatment. On the way home, Diva started pulling very insistently in a direction we never walk. I looked up to see our friend Marion, bundled up against the frigid 25 mph winds, out for her morning walk. Marion carries dog treats on her morning walks for all of her friends, and Diva can spot her from a mile away. We walked over and wished Marion a belated 95th birthday, and she told me how important it was to her to get outside today because she had been cooped up inside all day on her birthday because of the near-zero temperatures.

As we left Marion and continued on our way home, I was surprised to notice how much my spirits were lifted. I felt as if I had just won the lottery. I hadn't even noticed how deflated I was until talking with Stephanie and Marion.

Being the highly adaptable creatures we are, somehow we have managed to find ways to cope with this awful plague—at least, those of us who have not died or been impaired for life. I'm adapting, I'm doing OK, but boy, I can't wait to sit on the porch with my neighbors for an hour or so, talking about absolutely nothing. ▼

References

Morris, D. (1969). *The naked ape.* New York: Dell.

A version of this article originally appeared on psychologytoday.com (Weiss, Jan 19, 2022, The underestimated pain of isolation).

Rhona Engels

Rhona Engels, lcsw, acsw, has been in private practice for 38 years. She feels lucky to be in a profession in which she gets to have significant and intimate conversations with people she comes to love and helps to change, and who have changed her. She agrees with Adam Phillips that "psychotherapy is a conversation worth having if it shows us aspects of ourselves that we didn't know we could value."
rhonae1@gmail.com

The Thing With Feathers

Soon after fleeing COVID infested New York City for the Catskill Mountains, I started taking photographs, mostly of nature. In the process, I began to notice that certain photos haunt me, eliciting powerful feelings, musings, and memories.

Alder Lake, late Summer 2020, Catskills

This photo, for instance, of Alder Lake, about 15 miles from the house where husband Steve and I are staying, evokes warmth, comfort, longing, and sadness, summoning memories of many summers of family life at our country home on Petit Lac Long in the Laurentian Mountains north of Montreal. We moved many times while I was growing up, but our country home, the soul of our family, remained until it was sold 2 years before my father died, when I was 54. The lake was so much part of my life that it seemed part of me. I don't ever recall using shower or bathtub. Soap and shampoo sat on the steps leading down to the water and we dipped in and out through the days and evenings. Summer beginnings were marked by the first shock of a cold swim. Early morning, when my father was in residence from the city for the weekend, I would startle awake as he shut the front door just under my bedroom window. Throwing on my swimsuit I'd run down the stairs to join him for the first swim of the day. Wordless, we'd stand in the cold water, rose-gold mist around our ankles, taking deep breaths before diving in, then swimming silently, surrounded by strands of sunrise mist.

No wonder, then, that I took refuge in The Catskills, remarkably similar to the Laurentians. My daughter, who spent so many of those summers with me and her grandparents, knows this too. She and her family have a country home near Amber Lake, about 15 minutes from where we are, and have settled in since COVID.

Looking back at this photograph, Ingmar Bergman's (1957) film *Wild Strawberries* comes to mind. Professor Borg, played by the magnificent 78-year-old Victor Sjostrom (same age as me) is lying in bed unable to sleep, a very familiar condition to me these past 2 years. Traveling to the countryside of his childhood to receive an honorary degree has propelled the elderly doctor into an existential crisis, as he struggles to come to terms with the pleasures and failures of his life, particularly his emotional coldness and self-absorption which his daughter bitterly points out. In voiceover, the sympathetic narrator tells us that when the professor is worried or sad, he returns for comfort to the memories of his childhood.

Yes.

We then see him in his dream/memory, returned to his childhood country home, an old man, somewhat stooped, wearing a faded coat, and staring out at a lake very much like the one in my photograph and in my earlier life. A young woman in a flowing white dress approaches, the lost love of his life. She calls out to him to fetch his father to help pick wild strawberries for supper. "I can't find my parents," he says. "I'll help you," she replies, and guides him through a meadow to an opening through two trees overlooking a still and pristine lake. In the distance, Borg's father, much younger than he, is fishing, while his graceful young mother sits on the grass nearby. They wave to him, then turn away. Bergman shows us the old man's face in larger and larger closeup, softer, gentler, tender, glowing with forgiveness, compassion, sadness, regret, and a hint of reconciliation and redemption in the face of death. Sjostrom died 3 years after completion of this, his last film.

Sjostrom's face reminds me of my father's in old age, and as my face ages it seems to me that mine resembles his. During our final weekend at our country house, just after it was sold, I dreamt that I was looking out at the lake from our living room window, and in the distance I saw my father standing in our canoe, gliding west towards the sunset. I could tell, even before the house was actually sold, that he was gradually leaving. He seemed increasingly quiet and contemplative. One day, on a walk together, he mentioned that he had joined the Hemlock society. I quickly stopped him, joking that he was strong as a horse and likely to live many more years. Of course I knew but didn't want to know, that I was afraid and already grieving, but still, that memory makes me cringe with regret. I feel this especially now that I am the age he was then, moving west into the fall and winter of my life, and longing for others to understand and perhaps share my fear of dying as I believe he wished from me. I'll never know, but it occurs to me that perhaps he wanted me to express my fears about what would happen to me after he died, so that he could comfort me.

Farmstead stone walls along the Beaverkill River, Fall 2020, Catskills

As a child, I not only feared my parents' deaths but also my own. My dying meant never again looking out at the sun glinting on the lake, never again seeing the grass snakes sunning themselves on the stone wall facing the water. When I was about 10, I remember standing outside our house at night. Back then, ambient light was minimal, so the sky was a deep velvet black dotted with billions of stars, the Milky Way a thick white cloud arched across the sky, the lake a black mirror. Gazing up, I felt the hugeness, indifference, and eternity of what would remain unchanged long after I was dead. This gave me great comfort.

Palmer Hill Trail, Winter 2021, Catskills

Hiking in the Catskills for over 2 years now, I've witnessed the beauty of winter on trees, the branches and dead leaves like white lace, transforming to green, then yellow, and back again to white...permanence in change. The comfort I felt at 10, in 1953, that same sense of a vast eternity in the face of childhood turmoil, grief, and fear of death, my need of consolation from nature I find again in hiking, swimming, my photographs, and the memories they evoke. This seems oddly true whether the memories are happy or sad.

Many memories bring back good feelings. Fall in the Laurentians meant we were no longer living in our house, just visiting on weekends. Swimming was no longer possible, so I spent hours on our living room couch staring out at the lake to the mountains on the other side. I followed the minute changes of color as a faint lightening of green gave way to glorious bursts of deep red, bright orange, and golden yellow in contrast with the dark green/black evergreens, standing stiff and tall among the birch and maple trees. Such joyous beauty from dying leaves resembling flowers, a burst of joy before the long sleep of winter.

Frick Pond, Fall 2020, Catskills

In the following photograph, here I am 68 years later at Big Pond instead of Petit Lac Long, 390 miles away, staring out at the fall leaves of the mountains beyond. Everything has changed, yet right now, looking at this photograph, I could be 10 years old, awed, comforted, and content.

Other memories bring back painful feelings. At 10, I had already accumulated a certain amount of unhappiness. My parents fought, often viciously and without resolution. My mother provided wonderful food and had a finely tuned mind, along with resentment and regret that she had been trapped in motherhood, which the times required but she secretly didn't want. She was often critical, impatient, irritable, or withdrawn. I gave up on her early in my life and turned to my father. Jekyll-and-Hyde like, he could be encouraging and loving, but when offended, he got enraged, vengeful, mean, and sometimes violent, especially with one of my two brothers. Love from him was like reading Shakespeare by lightning: unpredictable, wonderful, and suddenly transformed into rage. Not surprising that I turned to nature as comfort for hurt and loneliness.

Big Pond, Fall 2021, Catskills

Even in the company of my two brothers, nearby grandparents, uncles, aunts and cousins, I was frequently lonely in the Laurentians. Depending on your point of view, my parents gave us freedom or neglected us, though they also provided us with a love of music and spirited conversation about politics, justice, and literature and with wonderful meals. I have very warm, happy memories of our extended family, about 30 of us, gathering with great good cheer every weekend on the grounds of our house, swimming, eating, and laughing. I learned trust in my body and in the wilderness that surrounded us. However, I also recall great stretches of time spent alone with my dog, wandering the woods without ever having to be concerned that my parents might wonder where I was. This gave me a sense both of freedom and the loneliness of their indifference. The natural world kept me company.

In this photograph below, husband Steve is vertically rooted against the horizontals of water, mountains, and sky. He stands out all the more for being in shadow, enveloped by the nature that surrounds him. And indeed, his love of nature is very much part of him and something we share. In this photograph, it is as if I have let him into my private world of nature.

Big Pond, Fall 2021, Catskills

More and more, though, COVID, the great revealer, has made me realize to what extent my lifelong turn to the beauty and permanence of nature has been an illusion. This has nothing to do with nature itself. It has everything to do with us humans. Of course, I'd have to be beyond redemption if I wasn't already aware of our overwhelming destructiveness. Yet, the pandemic seems more starkly to expose the dark side of the human race. Freud (1930) believed that in opposition to eros, the drive toward survival, propagation, sex, and other creative, life-producing drives, we have a death drive:

> The meaning of the evolution of civilization...must present the struggle between Eros and Death, between the instinct of life and the instinct of destruction, as it works itself out in the human species. This struggle is what all life essentially consists of, and the evolution of civilization may therefore be simply described as the struggle for life of the human species. (p. 77)

Everywhere I look, I see the evidence: in the extreme individualism and cruelty of our politics, in racial and socio-economic injustice, in corruption of money and power. Above all else, who could have predicted that COVID would peel back layers of denial to help confirm Freud's belief? We have the ability and apparently the drive to engineer our own extinction along with all of nature as we know it.

As a child in the Laurentians, I could never sleep past 6:00 a.m. because of the loud, joyous cacophony of birds. When I last visited 2 years ago, I was struck by the eerie morning silence, just a bird call here, a few chirps there. Writing this article, I checked it out. Zaller (2020) cites a 2019 study by Rosenberg et al that confirms "widespread population decline of birds over the past half century, resulting in the cumulative loss of billions of breeding individuals across a wide range of species and habitats" (Zaller, p. 159). Of course this is also true of many species of plants and animals. A 2019 United Nations report states that "just over a decade is all that remains to stop irreversible damage from climate change," citing General Assembly President María Fernanda Espinosa Garcés declaring further that "we are the last generation that can prevent irreparable damage to our planet" (United Nations, 2019).

That's about 7 years from now.

Human destructiveness is not news. However, wars may end, and, hopefully, we have learned to hold back use of our most destructive weapons. Yet, with all the science and technology we have at hand, with all the best knowledge mirroring back to us our dash to extinction, we are nonetheless rushing towards a self-created annihilation of our species and all life as we have known it.

Adam Phillips (1994) observes that "depression is a self-cure for the terrors of aliveness, of being alive to one's losses and therefore to one's desires" (p. 82). The destruction we are raining down on all of nature and ultimately ourselves makes me realize that underneath the elegiac tone of my photographs and memories is a reluctance to come alive to my own terrors, to the impossible task of integrating too many losses--of anticipated experiences, of so little time left, of faith in my fellow humans and the future, guilt for my heedless contribution to the mess, fear, sadness, and anger for the world my daughter, grandchildren, and the great grandchildren I will never know will inherit if they can even live on a planet that may no longer support them.

In exposing so many stark realities and losses, I think the pandemic has disrupted my, perhaps our, capacity to mourn. With so many losses in the present along with fears and doubts about the future, it makes sense that I would seek consolation in the past that itself turns out to be part illusion. What remains just as true as when I was 10 is that the stars will live on according to the laws of the universe, immune to our destructiveness. That, however, is a pretty low bar of consolation, when everything alive on our planet is at our mercy.

The pandemic induced loss of so many experiences I was anticipating at this point in my life, along with the ugly realities COVID has exposed, are too much to mourn. I need witnesses. For some of my patients, young people involved in the climate or political justice movements, listening to their determination, despair, and resilience, I hope my witnessing helps them carry on. Certainly, whether they know it or not, they help me find purpose in helping them. Perhaps I am writing this article, sharing these photographs, memories, grief, and anger because I need witnesses, fellow travelers to mourn with me so that I can be alive to my losses, to come fully alive to all of it, which allows for more joy, with or without hope.

Afterword

Sharing my photographs has made me realize that it is only in the company of others that I get surprised out of myself and tickled by something new. I showed the photograph below to a good friend. His reaction helped me grasp that my photographs don't just summon up the past for me. They are my attempt to create something of meaning and pleasure in the present, something new that can be interpreted differently by others. To me this tree, which I have now seen many times in all seasons, had conveyed resilience and determination in pandemic times. My friend had another reaction. He said, "I like the octopus tree. Surely I'm not the first one to ask: Do the roots move at night?"

Alder Lake, Fall 2021, Catskills

"Hope" is the thing with feathers

Hope is the thing with feathers -
That perches in the soul -
And sings the tune without the words -
And never stops - at all -

—Emily Dickinson

References

Bergman, I. (1957). *Wild strawberries.* Stockholm: Svensk Filmindustri.

Freud, S. (1930). *Civilization and its discontents.* (James Strachey, Trans.) (1961). New York: W. W. Norton & Company.

Philips, A. (1994). *On flirtation.* Cambridge, MA: Harvard University Press.

United Nations. (2019). Only 11 years left to prevent irreversible damage from climate change, speakers warn during General Assembly high-level meeting. Meeting Coverage and Press Releases. 28 March 2019. Retrieved from https://www.un.org/press/en/2019/ga12131.doc.htm

Zaller, J. (2020). *Daily poison: Pesticides—an underestimated danger.* Cham, Switzerland: Springer International Publishing.

We must learn to awaken and keep ourselves awake, not by mechanical aid, but by an infinite expectation of the dawn.

—Henry David Thoreau

Once again,
the
trees are
about to show
us
the quiet
magic and
beauty
of new
beginnings.

—S.C. Lourie@butterfliesandpebbles

Jonathan Farber

Jonathan Farber practices and trains psychotherapists online and in Washington, DC, and Chapel Hill, NC. He has a PhD in clinical psychology from Duke but learned much more from his clients and his colleagues in the American Academy of Psychotherapists. In an age when people are increasingly identified and flattened into whatever group they belong to, he's grown a little obsessed with defending the role of psychotherapy in honoring the complex uniqueness of the individual. He loves to hear from readers and can be reached at *Jonathan.Farber@gmail.com.*

A Beacon of Hope?

Darkness was one of the many things that frightened me as a child. In pools of darkness, my imagination seethed and curdled endlessly. I could see monsters of every description taking form in the closet, and the floor of my room swarmed with fanged and spiny creatures who kept me from running down the hall to the safety of my parents' room, where I knew I'd be lovingly received, but I also knew I'd hear fatigue and impatience in their voices. Little nightlights were my islands of security, and—except when their bulbs burnt out, another perpetual worry—they enabled me to relax enough to savor the escape into sleep, at least until the horrors in my dreams sent me fleeing right back into consciousness.

Somewhere along the way, I learned to steamroll over my fears and do most of what I wanted in spite of them: use shampoo that stung my eyes, play competitive sports, talk to girls, put my thoughts on paper, travel to strange places, eat strange foods (well, maybe I'm still working on that last one). But when my children were uncomfortable turning out their lights at night, I related, and they were met with total acceptance and support.

"That's fine. Do you want the light on by your bed, or the big ceiling light, or the light in the hall? Or all three?" Whatever they wanted, not an issue. And each of my four children did indeed have fears of his or her own. And we grew accustomed to leaving the hall light on, so much so that when the last child was in high school, my wife and I rarely thought to turn off the light in the upstairs hall until we were in bed, exhausted, and irritable.

"Shouldn't you have gotten it? You were the last one to come upstairs."

"But I thought you were going back down. I left it on for you."

So nobody turned out the light, night after night and—too tired to get up—I'd descend sourly into sleep trying to do the math and determine how much money we were wasting: figuring 7 hours per night times 365 times 8 cents per kw hour, and why don't I ever remember to look up the wattage on that compact fluorescent, but let's call it 18...

Enter the COVID pandemic. We barely saw our neighbors, not even the nearest ones, a warm and sociable couple in their 80s, whose house was just barely visible through the woods. We'd heard that the husband, Dan, a midwestern farm boy who'd discovered his talent for math and spent a career as a university professor, was in treatment for some kind of scary blood cancer, and we worried about them sometimes but never really spoke. Finally, in one of those illusory respites when we thought the pandemic was winding down, we had them over for dinner. Dan was apparently finished with his treatment, which had gone extremely well.

At one point he interrupted our usual conversation, about the sorry state of the world, to comment for the first time directly about his recent illness. His voice still had his cheery midwestern inflection, though, like the rest of us, he looked a little older, a little more haggard, and his voice was a little raspier. He said it felt important to tell us something, and we all quieted and listened.

He said the treatment had been difficult and frightening and that he often couldn't sleep at night, and he'd feel terribly alone. But whenever he'd look out his window—even at 2:00 or 3:00 in the morning—he'd see through the woods that our light was still on. He knew someone else was out there, awake too, and it made him feel he had company, he said, and he pictured our son up late poring over his studies, building his future, and it gave him hope. "It told me I was going to be OK. I know it doesn't make sense, but that's really how I felt."

What? My wife and I looked at each other; we didn't know what to say.

"I'm glad it was helpful to you," I offered vaguely.

"That must have been such a difficult time," said Nancy.

"I just needed you to know," he said.

I realized later how much it reminded me of times my patients have told me they benefited greatly from something I hardly realized I was doing and never expected would be helpful. It's difficult to know what to say. I don't want to dismiss or minimize something clearly meaningful to somebody else, but I feel awkward or even fraudulent taking credit for something unintentional. Sometimes I look for a middle ground, partially acknowledging my surprise. Sometimes I just avoid the issue until the moment passes, and then regret my silence. But in a life where I sometimes harm others without intending to, maybe it's a nice counterbalance to know that sometimes I help others unintentionally, too.

Dan's comment also triggered the final step in the slow transformation of my attitude about hope. I used to think of hope as simply a belief, a purely cognitive experience: the belief that the current drama will go well. I couldn't understand why people made such a fuss about a belief about the future. What's the big deal? You'll either be right or wrong, and you'll find out when you get there.

Over time, I've come to see hope as something more emotional, as a particular style of stepping forward into the fearsome uncertainty of the future. I've seen many people who live with hope and, other things being equal, they are better off than those who live without it. If Dan had had hope, and his treatment failed, and he died, the months with hope would still have been a better way for him to live through that time. It's like the truth-loving philosopher in me and the people-loving parent/psychotherapist in me disagree, and for now, I've made my choice. I'll be the therapist. I'm now pro-hope.

Will it last?

We can only hope.

> Never deprive someone of hope; it might be all they have.
>
> —H. Jackson Brown, Jr.

> The road that is built in hope is more pleasant to the traveler than the road built in despair, even though they both lead to the same destination.
>
> —Marion Zimmer Bradley, *The Fall of Atlantis*

Linda Tillman

LINDA TILLMAN, PHD, lives in Atlanta, Georgia, where she is a beekeeper, quilter, and bread baker. She recently retired from her more than 30-year clinical psychology practice. Now she spends her time playing with her grandchildren, tending to her bees, and cooking for family and friends. She learned a lot from her mother, including the joy of feeding people well, the importance of imbuing one's craft with artistry, and the enhancement of life through observing nature.
linda.tillman@gmail.com

Hope, Rising

THE QUART-SIZED MASON JAR SITTING ON A LEDGE CAUGHT MY ATTENTION THE MINUTE I STEPPED ONTO THE SCREENED PORCH AT THE BACK OF MY MOTHER'S HOUSE. The contents were a blacker-than-black thick semi-liquid morass. It must have been sitting on that ledge for at least 3 years. I stared at the jar in horror. Even with no label on the jar, I knew exactly what it was.

The problem with cleaning out my mother's house after her death at 93 was that it was completely full of story-worthy items, but I wanted to throw everything away without looking at any of it. If I picked up clothing, all I could think about was how critical my mother was of my appearance, my clothing choices, my weight, my hair. If I read something my father had written, all I remembered was his pressure on all of us to be perfectly formed in his image. If I sat down in any room, all I thought of was how lonely and sad I felt in that house. I kept wishing lightning would strike during a Mississippi thunderstorm, burn the house to the ground, and free me from revisiting these bad memories.

My sister, going through drawers, offered me jewelry, scarves, linen handkerchiefs, and knick-knacks. I didn't want any of it, none of it at all.

But the black goo-filled jar sent me sprinting into the kitchen.

I held onto hope as I poured hot water around the top of the jar. Summoning all of my strength, I screwed off the corroded canning jar ring and pried off the lid with the tines of a fork. A smell worse than any sewer flooded into the room. Totally gross and beyond decrepit, the jar and its black interior drew me in, despite my feeling as if

I were staring into a dark tunnel without an end. But I was not daunted and began with great care to spoon the nasty black sludge out, one small bit at a time, tossing each gross tiny spoonful into the garbage disposal.

"Have you lost your mind?" asked my sister, pinching her nose shut as she raised every window in the kitchen and adjacent dining room. When that didn't seem to lessen the smell, she propped the doors open to the deck from both rooms. "What IS that?"

"Clearly it's hell in a jar," I said, never taking my focus from my task. My surgical precision worked. Miracle of miracles, in the very center of the jar, in the heart of the black smelly filth, was a small golf ball-sized mass of pure white. I picked up a clean spoon and lifted it out like I was trying not to break an egg.

In the center of that jar I had found gold: my mother's 150-year-old sourdough starter. I was determined to take it home to Atlanta intact.

Black decay still clung to the pure-white ball in smudges. I took a flour-sacking towel—there were always two or three dozen in my mother's kitchen—and gently dabbed away every black moldy area. Then I spooned what was left into a clean plastic sandwich bag, zipped it shut, and triple-bagged it. Even with the careful wiping away of the black decomposing gunk, I wasn't 100% sure that the rotting would stop. I wanted the sandwich bag to arrive in Atlanta with me. If the smell escaped, should the glob of starter continue to putrefy in my checked suitcase in the airplane hull, the starter might never return to my possession.

My mother wanted a boy when her first child was on the way, and I arrived instead. Not only was I a girl, but I needed glasses and was in so many ways a disappointment to her. She bonded with my younger brother who followed 2 years later and left me pretty much to figure out life on my own.

But in the eighth grade when the home-ec teacher assigned a 6-week end-of-the-year project, the process of completing it created a place where my mother and I would stand together for the rest of our lives. "Anything you want to cook," the teacher said to the room full of girls. "And I want a detailed report about whatever you make. It's your final project—due in 6 weeks."

"You could try baking bread," my mother suggested. I loved this idea. Bread baking sounded like fun, and it was something my mother had also always wanted to learn to do. My grandmother had taught my mother to make delicious biscuits and perfect, buttermilk-light cornbread but not yeast bread.

First, we went to the bookstore and bought two cookbooks: *The American Woman's Cookbook*, an encyclopedic volume with notches cut into the stacked pages (helpful for quickly finding the bread recipes), and a Sunset soft cover book with lots of photos of different types of loaves. Together we flipped through both books full of pages and pages of delicious sounding bread recipes.

For the next 6 Saturdays, my mother hung out in the kitchen with me as we learned how to make the yeast happy by feeding it a tiny bit of honey or sugar as we crumbled the cake of yeast into warm water. My mother did a lot for me—led a Girl Scout troop, made sure I had the right costumes for plays and pageants, found instructors to teach me piano and dancing—but this was the very first thing she had done with me.

"Start with the basics," my mother said, so I baked plain white bread the first week. We looked at the pictures in her old Betty Crocker cookbook and she helped me put my hands exactly where the photographed bakers had theirs. When the flour, water, salt, and the cake of yeast came together, my hands couldn't stop working with the mixture. The cookbook said the final dough should feel like a baby's bottom, and it did. Mother smiled at me and reached over to give the dough bottom an extra pat.

While the bread baked, we looked through the cookbooks to find the recipe for the next Saturday. My mother's oven didn't have a glass door, and opening the oven during the baking process risked ruining the loaves. I paced back and forth in front of the stove until the clock finally indicated that I could peek. The loaves were beautiful, warm brown in color, looking hard and soft at the same time. They had risen above the pan's edge in a perfect loaf shape. The tantalizing smell rushing out of the oven door filled the whole house.

When she and I cut the very first loaf, the smell circled my head, enveloping me, and the taste was unbelievably delicious. I had never tasted bread like that before, and from Mother's expression I could tell that she hadn't either.

Every Saturday, with my Brownie box camera, we took photos of the bread to put in my report. We each loved different breads. My favorite was the St. Lucia bread wreath, designed and baked to be worn on the head with lit candles for a festival in Sweden. I really wanted to light the candles but the idea of catching my hair on fire was a little scary. Balancing it on my head with the candles unlit, I posed for the photo.

My mother loved Monte Carlo bread, a white bread with currants. Long after my project was done and I had set my bread pans aside for teenaged fun, she began baking that Monte Carlo bread regularly. She tried a few other breads through the years but always had Monte Carlo bread in her freezer, wrapped to give away. She said, "A good cook is generous," and she lived by that. She gave bread to the friend who dropped by, to any repairman who came to work on something in the house, or to us kids to toast for breakfast. When she was stopped once for driving 35 mph in a 25-mph zone, the policeman only gave her a warning. She returned to the scene of the crime to take the forgiving cop a loaf of her Monte Carlo bread.

The feel of the dough and the charm of the loaves stayed with me always. I have baked bread almost every week of my adult life. While my mother's bread baking narrowed to Monte Carlo and the occasional sourdough loaf, I've continued experimenting with all kinds, shapes, and flavors of bread doughs, from ryes to sweet breads, from bagels to baguettes. I remember how people's faces looked when she handed them a loaf of bread as a gift, and now I get to see that too because I give away most of the bread I bake.

When I was 16, my mother expanded her repertoire. She ordered a 100-year-old sourdough starter, a culture of wild yeast, from San Francisco. Her favorite sourdough recipe came from California miners who carried their sourdough starter in their pockets, keeping it warm, as they traveled west searching for gold. She fed and nurtured her starter to keep it going strong and, until a few years before her death, kept it safely in the refrigerator when she wasn't using it.

When I saw the black and nasty gunk filling the bottle on the porch, I knew it was her sourdough starter—a starter so old that it had been developed by a California gold rush miner and now so neglected that it might not have survived that muck of deterioration. To stay healthy and alive, a sourdough starter requires regular care and feeding for the wild yeasts that live in it. If not in the refrigerator, it needs flour and water added every day. If this starter still could make bread rise, it would be a miracle after several years on her hot Mississippi screened porch.

I read once that microbes from a baker's hands become a part of her sourdough starter, along with microbes from everyone who has ever baked with it. Sourdough carries its history with it and reflects every person who has ever touched it. My mother was truly giving away a piece of herself when she gave someone a loaf of bread. And her microbes were contained in her sourdough starter.

I really wanted that starter to live and thrive, but I didn't know if it could be rejuvenated.

Back in my Atlanta kitchen, I divided the starter into eight or nine cereal bowls and added one-quarter cup of flour and one-quarter cup of water to each bowl. I covered the bowls with wet kitchen towels and left home to go to work. When I walked into my kitchen at the end of the work day, each of those sourdough starter samples had bubbled up and over the edges of its container. Desperate for food, the starter yeast, as it finally got nourishment from the flour, had gone rogue, had risen out of the bowl, and had crept all over my counter.

"It worked!" I shouted to my empty house. "It worked!" And then I started crying. I couldn't bring her back, but I could bring back the sourdough starter and have a part of her, perhaps the most important part of our relationship, with me. ▼

Remember, hope is a good thing, maybe the best of things, and no good thing ever dies.

—Stephen King

Out of your dry thorn opens a rose garden.

—Rumi

Days with Pippo

Mary de Wit

Kingsport, Tennessee
md@in2wit.com

Hi! I'm your devoted graphic designer. I have produced layouts, illustrations, photographs, and covers for *Voices* since 2003. Linda Tillman's article reminded me of several vignettes I propped with Pippo during the sourdough craze days of the pandemic.

Our youngest son was a toddler in the early 1990s. His favorite book was *Tom and Pippo's Day* by Helen Oxenbury, published in 1988. After studying Ms. Oxenbury's illustrations I sewed a Pippo out of fake fur, stuffing, and buttons—he became my son's beloved snuggle buddy.

I had the lonesome blues after the death of my mother, who had lived with us for 7 years. The mood was intensified by the initial sequestering period due to COVID-19, a time I spent working on our house and sorting through things we'd accumulated. I missed our sons, and seeing Pippo flung on a chair made me nostalgic for the days of

Our sourdough starter makes bread rise.
We feed it flour every day. It is our hungry pet.

Pippo stirs the sourdough before it runs over.
"Stop, little pot! Stop!"

wonder and appreciation in their childhoods. Pippo became a symbol of separation, a surrogate child. Posing him and posting daily on Facebook became a thoughtful practice for me to acknowledge the beauty and privilege of everyday activities.

The Reece Museum at East Tennessee University called for entries for a permanent collection featuring *Local Art in the Age of the 2020 Global Pandemic.* I gathered my first 50 posts into a book to submit as art, and *50 Days with Pippo* (de Wit, 2020) was juried into the permanent collection. Creating posts every day for over a year yielded enough material for seven books (sequels are *51 Days with Pippo* through *56 Days with Pippo,* each book is one page longer than the last) for children and children-at-heart. I've nearly completed a cookbook of the recipes featured in the books.

Working on this project gave me a sense of hope, play, and connection with friends and family who were all isolated, too, and I'm proud to spread this collection of upbeat silliness into the world. ▼

"Oh, no! Dough overflow!"
Pippo presumes a protective pose.

"This bread dough bulge is bigger than the bowl," brags Pippo. "Oh boy, I believe it's baking time!"

"Yeasties and bacteria gone wild!" pronounces Pippo.
"You beasties fooled around long enough. Time to shape up!"

References

de Wit, M. (2020). *50 Days with Pippo*. Kingsport, TN: in2Wit publishing/ amazon print-on-demand.

de Wit, M. (2020). *51 Days with Pippo*. Kingsport, TN: in2Wit publishing/ amazon print-on-demand

de Wit, M. (2020). *52 Days with Pippo*. Kingsport, TN: in2Wit publishing/ amazon print-on-demand

de Wit, M. (2020). *56 Days with Pippo*. Kingsport, TN: in2Wit publishing/ amazon print-on-demand

Oxenbury, H. (1988). *Tom and Pippo's Day*. Discovery Toys.

New Day by Giuliana Reed

Susan D. Berlin

SUSAN D. BERLIN, LICSW, CASAC, is a psychotherapist specializing in the treatment of addictions and trauma and is sober over 33 years. She is licensed in DC, MD, VA, NY, and WY and has an office in Georgetown, DC. Once a full-time in-person therapist, Susan now practices primarily virtually as she considers when to go back in-person, if at all. Susan also founded and manages The Capital Networking Group (CNG), a national listserv for addiction and mental health professionals.
Susan@SusanBerlin.com

My Transformation, Hope, and Wonder as I Leave the COVID Winters

the profound effects of the pandemic on my person, my life, my work

PRE-PANDEMIC, I WAS A BUSY, SOCIAL WOMAN. I thrived in my extroverted self, going out to dinner, theatre, concerts, and more. I loved travel and being on the go. Then came March 2020, and the world turned on its axis. Pre-COVID I would have said that I really enjoyed my life and being a psychotherapist, which sounds lovely yet uninteresting, at least compared to now.

Having no idea how long our lives would be altered by this virus that was attacking us, the pandemic began to change me. Three things happened, and they are all relational. First, I embarked on a new friendship with a woman I had known at a distance for some 20 years. We had one dinner the week before lockdown and thus decided to be each other's pandemic buddy. She became my Saturday night in-person date. Other than when I travel, which didn't resume until 2021, we have been together almost every Saturday night, playing roaring games of backgammon (over 400 of them) and cooking, talking, laughing, and watching movies. Mostly we are talking and interacting, not watching. This was the first gem that came from the pandemic: I gained a soul sister that will surely be for life. We are fiercely loyal to each other and devoted to bringing truth, joy, love, and spirit to each other's world.

Here is some history behind the second thing that changed me in the pandemic. I began my long career at the Caron Foundation, in Pennsylvania, working in an incredible 5-day group intensive experiential program in 1989, after I graduated. I have been in touch with a few of the folks that I worked with back then. When the pandemic hit, one of the women that I knew peripherally put together a Facebook Messenger group and asked if anyone was interested in a 12-Step meeting. The rest, as they say, is history. Nearly 2 years later, we still meet every Friday night and have become connected in ways we couldn't have imagined. These people became my soul family, my tribe, and an integral part of my week and my life.

So, you see where this is going. As a result of this meeting (not long after its inception), I decided to put out an offering to the American Academy of Psychotherapists (AAP) for a 12-Step support group. Participation would not require being in a 12-Step program, but the meeting would be run in the format of 12-Step. We now have ten people, some who were previously in 12-Step and some who never were, but found their way to one because of our group, who have also become extended soul family and tribe members. This beautiful group includes a few people that I knew before but mostly people that I didn't know at all, who have now entered my life so fully, every week, and I imagine will be a part of it for a long time.

The third thing that transpired: During this time I left my long-term AAP peer group ("family group"). There was no contention; no one was at fault. It was an organic conclusion based on what I had come to understand that I needed and wanted. Let me explain.

I have lived my life mostly single and really wanting more primary people in it. I have wanted a tribe but hadn't found one, not even in AA. Although my family group helped me to feel like I had a tribe in AAP, I didn't have much with them outside of the Academy, and during the pandemic there was great resistance to meeting with any more regularity. I started my family group about 14 years ago; I think that's what we figured out. It was to be one of those groups that doesn't meet a ton throughout meetings...hahaha. It was an excellent group that held all of the wonderful, painful, acting out, joyful, character-raising dynamics that hopefully happen in most family/peer groups. I worked on so much of my character and my family of origin issues there. I really grew and came to know myself better. But growth also happened exponentially through the pandemic, outside of the group. As I got my tribe needs filled elsewhere, it became clearer to me that the gap was widening with my family group and that it was time to depart. It was sad to do that virtually and not in person, but it also seemed fitting somehow and was not belabored. My group understood my reasons, although they may not have liked that I was leaving (or they may have, in some way; it is family group after all). Collectively we could see that I had been asking for more, and that wasn't able to happen.

During the last 2 years, I became more of an introvert. I practiced self-care in a way that has been so fulfilling, so spiritual and loving. I relish the relationships developed and feel devoted to all that long-term friendships have and hold. I did not feel lonely; I just didn't. I felt in company with so many. I felt relieved of all the social pressures of my big life. I felt and feel much more discriminating about who I spend time with and what I do with my time. I am more relational (hard to believe that I could be more relational) and much choosier about who, what, where, and when.

Guess what, there is even more transformation that happened with me through the pandemic: I turned 60, became much more emotionally regulated, and fell in love with psychotherapy. "Really?" you might ask. Yup, really. I had never loved it the way so many do. I liked it a lot, and I was good at it, but something changed in going through the pandemic experience with people. I love working from home. I love being in my home, which when one is so busy one tends not to be so much. I love being with my cats, who are seniors, and I dare say they have loved having me there with them day after day. I love seeing people in their homes or vacation houses—or closets because it's the only place they could get privacy. I love seeing the guitar in the background, never knowing that they were musical because it never came up, until I could see it. I relish that we have been in a common experience, a giant, world-wide, collective experience—a trauma, a healing, a surviving, a dying—all together. I am an insane optimist and can reliably find the good, the rich, the delicious in the most distasteful of circumstances, while constantly being present to the total truth, the pain and suffering as well.

I will never go back to full-time in-person practice. I have always had some number of virtual patients, but now I will be more flexible with that because of the ease with which it allows us to be together. Very few people missed therapy due to work meetings, traffic, or other things that would have normally gotten in the way. They were here, with me, week after week, without fail, to a point that was almost exhausting. The work changed and got deeper as a result of that. Sure, there are limitations, but there are also benefits. What I don't get to see because we are not in person, I get to find in other ways through the screen. I don't think I would have explored the myriad of relationships with pets, for example, that people have, that are of paramount importance.

I am not saying here that I did not feel scared, even petrified at times. It was a trauma, what we have all been through, and I had to process the same trauma in other people's lives with them day after day, hour after hour, while processing it in my own. It was painful and exhausting, but it was also enlivening. It was truly and wholly relational; we were in it together. That has been an incredible experience.

I wouldn't change anything about the last 2 years—not that we can, of course, but we do like to play with that thought in our busy creative minds. I have landed in myself, as a woman, as a 60-year-old, as a friend, and as a psychotherapist. That would not have happened without the circumstances of the last 2 years. It is true always that life changes us. That has been my experience before, but these last 2 years stand out as a supreme example of that, and for that I am grateful. I am a person who believes in change, who believes that I can change, even in the moments when I feel the most hopeless in the appearance of yet another character challenge. This spring, as I awaken with this formulation of a rebirth and a blooming, I turn my head to the sun and say, "Bring it, baby. I have faith in myself and in those I love to find our way, and I am finding my way each day, every day. And that is hopeful!" ▼

Resurrection

Joanna Frederick

It starts with the smell of smoke.
Then the roar of the flames.
Yes, there is pain.
This time it was even the catalyst,
the latest arsonist.

The cycle ends by burning myself into the ground.

Followed by an effusive nothingness
Devoid of connection
To self or others.
No room even for regret.
Mind shattering silence.

A pile of smoldering ashes.
Ashes can hold no future can they?
Is it really over this time?

And then, a stirring.
A rising.
I can breathe again.

Spreading my wings to try them out.

This phoenix is starting to get her feathers back.

Kristie Nies

KRISTIE NIES, PHD, is a board-certified neuropsychologist, psychotherapist, and certified yoga instructor. Recent personal and world events have inspired her to foster resilience in the face of despair.
krisnies@gmail.com

Resilience: Hope in Action

You kept faith when you didn't have a prayer
Found hope when it wasn't even there
—From the song "Love is Stronger" by Jason Crabb

IN MARCH OF 2020, THE THREAT OF COVID-19 WAS IN THE AIR AND ON THE AIR WAVES NONSTOP. What started as a daily death count, with sporadic honoring of individuals, morphed into a rolling statistic that churned ever upward until the numbers themselves became meaningless. Elective medical procedures were limited, and family members were restricted from accompanying or visiting their loved ones whose procedures had been approved or who were on their deathbed.

Amidst this emotional climate, I fell off of a bicycle. Through the combination of inexperience and ignorance, I failed to remove my foot from the toe clip and simply fell over. In revisiting the accident, I was reminded of the '60s variety show *Laugh-In* (Schlatter, 1967), which featured a character played by the late Arte Johnson. He rode a child-sized tricycle and inexplicably tipped over. This gag recurred throughout the season and became humorous over time. Although I was riding a 10-speed bicycle, the image is apropos. The distance between perpendicular and parallel was short but irrelevant, as I landed on another bicycle. The result was a smashed humerus and the need for surgery. After several alienating and painful hours in the emergency department, I was released home with my arm in a sling and instructed to await an appointment with an orthopedic surgeon. I literally sat up for 24 hours, unable to find a position in which I could sleep. The surgery was considered urgent, but because of COVID restrictions, was postponed for 4 very long days.

I have a self-sufficient streak that runs deep in my soul, compliments of a dismissive attachment style. Following surgery, I was in a sling for 6 weeks and slept in a recliner for 3 months. I was out of work for 5 months. I couldn't easily bathe, dress, or feed myself. (The only thing worse than not having the generous support of my partner during this time was having it.) The confrontation with dependency was like a punch to a bruise. Given that the unspoken ethos of my family of origin included independence at all costs, I felt diminished. But even more devastating than the physical reality was increased awareness of the fragility of my bones. A new trepidation toward life challenged my usual frontier spirit.

I was diligent with my range of motion exercises and determined to have an exceptional recovery. I discovered there were limits to what I could will to happen. "Well, it was a salvage procedure," the physical therapist said rather off-handedly, referring to the procedure of reverse shoulder replacement. "It's what they do when they can't do anything else." And while that sentiment may have been true, hearing those words in my vulnerable state left me feeling gut-punched. Tears threatened to expose my distress, and I left mid-session with the simple admission, "I can't." I sought more treatment, but was summarily dismissed because I'd had such a "good" recovery. I continued to resist this conclusion. In my mind, it wasn't good. Months after the fact, my struggle to come to terms with the limitations imposed by the surgery and the injury itself created inertia. I alternated between denial and dissociation. Since I was unable to return to work, I had the gift of time, but I couldn't open the package.

Resilience, Arianna Huffington's (2020) word of the year for 2020, has become a topic of interest for me personally and professionally. One definition of the word is the ability to bounce back from adversity. My definition of bouncing back included full use of my arm. I am a middle-class American with resources and a can-do attitude, yet I failed to meet my goal. My own springiness in doubt, with bitterness brewing, I began to question the entire concept. Maybe resilience as a cultural ethos is merely the result of excessive publicity. In this age of fake news and politicized science, I began to look for reasons to believe the hype in order to salvage hope.

Some people go through unimaginable pain and suffering and not only survive but eventually thrive, while others flounder in despair. What is the secret to flourishing despite adversity? It turns out that how our brains learn to handle stress determines resilience. While there are studies of the effects of oppression on certain groups of people, it is difficult to conduct a human study of resilience prospectively. However, animal models provide insight about mechanisms underlying resilience. Neuroscience uses a social defeat model (Pena, Nestler, & Bagot, 2019) to study stress in rodents. A mouse is placed in physical contact with an aggressor mouse for a few minutes a day and then housed behind a screen in the same cage as the aggressor for the rest of the day. This activity is repeated for 10 days. In this type of stress paradigm, most mice develop symptoms comparable to depression in humans (i.e., social avoidance, loss of interest in sugar water, high desire for cocaine water). All of the mice were agitated by the stressor, but one-third of them were considered naturally resilient because they did not develop mouse depression. Scientists concluded that the difference between groups had to do with neuroplasticity, the ability of the brain to change. Naturally resilient mice regulated more genes than did the vulnerable mice (i.e., turned on specific neurochemical switches in reward circuitry that counteracted the stress) and prevented social avoidance and loss of pleasure. That is, they tapped into their genetic code to alter their own internal pharmacy. While there is undoubtedly a genetic predisposition toward resilience, it is not a fixed trait. Rather, it is a dynamic process. I believe that most people can learn to actively use brain power to foster resilience and counteract stress and adversity.

Nietzsche (and singer/songwriter Kelly Clarkson) tell us that what doesn't kill us makes us stronger. In fact, research (Seery, Holman, & Silver, 2010) shows that some adversity (relative to no adversity or high adversity) results in less emotional distress and higher life satisfaction. This aphorism is related to two versions of what Jonathan Haidt (2006) calls the adversity hypothesis. The weak version states that "adversity *can* lead to growth, strength, joy, and self-improvement" (p. 141) while the strong version states that "people *must* endure adversity, and that the highest levels of growth and development are only open to those who have to face and overcome great adversity" (p. 143). The weak version reportedly has empirical support but little in the way of guidance. Research for the strong version is lacking, but Haidt finds fault with experimental designs. He believes researchers have been looking for confirmation of the benefit of enduring hardship in the wrong part of the self (e.g., basic traits). He believes the biggest bang for the adversity buck occurs when a narrative (which he cites psychologist Dan McAdams defining as "an evolving story that integrates a reconstructed past, perceived present, and anticipated future into a coherent and vitalizing life myth") is revised (p. 143). The revision process is an essential feature of sensemaking. Fortunately, our brains were born for the task. The integration of our experiences is where we learn to thrive. When events create opportunities, the process of sensemaking results in brain change and hopefully resilience.

Haidt (2006) stipulates that during a crisis people respond in three ways. They use direct action, cognitive reframing, or avoidance. He describes optimists as revisionist historians who respond to crisis with a coping style that alternates between direct action and reappraisal. If direct action fails, benefits are sought, the chapter is rewritten. Pessimists, rather than taking action to address a problem, expend their efforts minimizing pain. Through the lens of a pessimist, resilience cannot gain traction, and life is deemed unfair. Despair becomes self-perpetuating. Apparently, the key to post-traumatic growth is not optimism per se but the aforementioned ability to make sense of things. Optimists simply find this an easier task than do pessimists. Finally, to benefit from adversity, action is required. Haidt insists that all of the following pursuits are necessary: (a) change your cognitive style (if you are not an optimist), (b) cherish and build a social support network, (c) find and practice religious faith, and (d) start writing.

One of the keys to behavioral change (e.g., diet, exercise) is identifying a motivator. Ironically, I am motivated by fear and often have to pick the lesser of two evils (e.g., fragile osteoporotic bones or a treatment that has rare but devastating side effects). In a similar vein, I am motivated to maintain a healthy lifestyle to avoid neurological complications (i.e., dementia). A byproduct of a healthy lifestyle is a resilient brain. My motivation for cognitive change is peace of mind. While no one would ever mistake me for an optimist, I am practicing to increase my characterological repertoire to include a rosy outlook. I liken this practice to a sport involving the equivalent of wind sprints, strength training, scrimmages, and Gatorade victories. I hit the wall with direct action to improve my range of motion, and some of my efforts may have caused more harm than good. No more wind sprints. The reappraisal included strengthening other aspects of arm function. I created several intricate colored pencil drawings and began knitting a sweater. I started playing the piano again. These activities are good for my arm and good for my brain. The scrimmages were internal. I had to use the cognitive behavioral technique of thought stopping to battle excessive rumination that started with "If only I'd..." and ended with "Why didn't I..." The victories, which generalize to my life as a whole, are subtle and perhaps only noticed in retrospect. For example, I recently got relocated from an aisle seat to a middle seat in the back of the plane for a very long flight. I was able to mute my reactivity. Rather than bemoaning my bad luck and pouting, I reminded myself that I was not walking barefoot across Guatemala with all of my belongings on my back. (I still went to great lengths, more due to persistence than hope, to get moved back to an aisle seat.)

Applying the remainder of Haidt's recommendations has been more straightforward. I am an introvert by inclination and by heritage, so even thinking about increasing my social support network created discomfort. Nevertheless, I invited myself to a book club. I know on an intellectual level that social interaction is beneficial. I am hoping that the camaraderie will eventually outweigh the awkwardness and anxiety so that I can experience the benefit on an emotional level as well. I chose to take the recommendations for religious faith and practice somewhat liberally, thus including yoga. I have renewed my passion for teaching a mind-body class, albeit online, for a group of friends. And finally, as evidenced by this article, I am writing.

One of my favorite ways to foster optimism (and therefore hope and resilience) is through the use of affirmations, the process of reflecting on important personal values or attributes. Some readers may recall the old *Saturday Night Live* (Michaels, 1975) character Stuart Smalley and his daily affirmations. One of his catch phrases was, "I'm good enough, I'm smart enough, and doggone it, people like me." While these skits were satire, designed to mock the self-help movement, affirmations have been shown to lead to reduced physiological responses to stress and to improve performance. Instagram has become a source of affirmations and inspiration for me. For example, the following meme from an unknown author needs no scientific validation: "New approach to self-care: Talk to myself the same way I talk to dogs. Hey sweet girl! Look at that beautiful belly! You're so clever. Want a treat?"

Effort and determination are generally considered positive, especially if the purpose is winning or beating the odds. Certainly, the dogged pursuit of a goal might reflect resilience. However, I would argue that choosing not to do something is also a sign of resilience. Consider Simone Biles and Naomi Osaka, professional athletes who opted out of major events in favor of their mental health. They were lauded by some and villainized by others on social media. Their choices to do battle in the arena of public opinion may have taken more determination than competing in their respective events.

This injury changed my life. Eventually, I returned to my job as lead neuropsychologist for a major health system. I know that I carry a little bit of shame about the accident, and it may have affected my leadership style, but I also know that the workplace climate had changed. Not only did my co-workers' work load increase because of me, I was not there to unite in battle against the workplace changes associated with COVID. Whatever the cause, I felt invisible to my co-workers and disrespected by administration. The void my absence had created was filled with toxic dynamics and resentment. My efforts toward good will were routinely thwarted, and I felt ineffectual. My response roughly followed the guidance of the Serenity Prayer. I could not accept what the job had become, and my efforts to change the situation had failed, so I changed what I could. I resigned and took a new position at another organization. Or perhaps my inspiration came from the old Kenny Rogers song, "The Gambler": "You got to know when to hold 'em, know when to fold 'em..." (Schlitz, 1976).

I have come to believe that resilience is hope in action. Like so many things in life, it is a unique process that varies by person and situation. It is neither linear nor static, but rather an active process of negotiating situational demands. It includes surviving with grace, with an eye for preventing wear and tear on the soul. It is the art of the climb. I can't say that I am searching for the good I can derive from my injury, but I am hoping something positive will emerge that will not feel pyrrhic. Until then, I will embrace a heroic victory and sum up my current narrative with a tweet from Ebonee Davis (2017) : "The habits you created to survive will no longer serve you when it's time to thrive. Get out of survival mode. New habits. New life." ▼

References

Davis, E. (2017, September 20). *The habits you created to survive will no longer serve you when it's time to thrive. Get out of survival mode. New habits. New life.* [Tweet]. Twitter. https://twitter.com/eboneedavis/status/910485863590764545?lang=en

Haidt, J. (2006). *The happiness hypothesis: Finding modern truth in ancient wisdom.* New York: Basic Books.

Huffington, A. (2020). And the word of the year is...resilience. *Thrive.* 2020, December 4. Retrieved from https://thriveglobal.com/stories/arianna-huffington-resilience-word-of-the-year-2020/

Michaels, L. (Creator and Executive Producer). (1975). Daily affirmations with Stuart Smalley. *Saturday Night Live* [TV series]. Broadway Video.

Pena, C.J, Nestler, E. J., & Bagot, R.C. (2019). Environmental programming of susceptibility and resilience to stress in adulthood in male mice. *Frontiers of Behavioral Neuroscience.* March 01. https://doi.org/10.3389/fnbeh.2019.00040

Schlatter, G. (Executive Producer). (1967). *Rowan & Martin's Laugh-In* [TV series]. George Schlatter-Ed Friendly Productions.

Schlitz, D. (1976). The gambler [Song, recorded by K. Rogers]. On *The gambler* [album]. Nashville, TN: United Artists Group. November 1978.

Seery, M. D., Holman, E. A., & Silver, R. C. (2010). Whatever does not kill us: Cumulative lifetime adversity, vulnerability, and resilience. *Journal of Personality and Social Psychology, 99*(6), 1025–1041. https://doi.org/10.1037/a0021344

The Upward Spiral

Joanna Frederick

What if in all of this
There's a story I could tell you
Of a body rendered painful
Due to faulty connective tissue

It's genetic they say,
Something you've always had
I look fine on the outside
Surely, it can't be that bad

A darkness fell over me
My spirit felt under threat
Losing pieces of myself
As I watched my sun set

A deep dive into the neuroscience of pain
Has taught me that feeling fear
Fires up similar neural circuits
Leaving the solution further unclear

Like a doll being disassembled
A doctor for each body part
When it's looking like healing
Needs to also involve my heart

Enter a motley crew of characters
Who breathe hope back into me
A cast of healers and mischief makers
Who show me the path to being free

While feeling broken and scared
I still find the strength to fight
Knowing that there are sorcerers
To guide me out of this plight

Move this way, no, that way
Watch them scrape away the pain
Sending messages of safety
Like water to the fire in my brain

Becoming like a temporary family
Cheering me on to the finish line
Ensuring that deep down I can know
Somehow again my sun will shine

My Hope for Psychotherapy's Contribution to Healing the World

John Rhead, PhD

Baltimore, Maryland
jrheadphd@gmail.com

These days I think of psychotherapy as an interpersonally facilitated quest in search of wisdom. Wisdom I define as the knowledge of (a) that which brings happiness and fulfillment and (b) that which brings pain and regret. Some wisdom is universal and applies to all humans, and some is idiosyncratic. It is important to acquire both.

The psychotherapist is on a life-long quest for wisdom and uses encounters with clients as an opportunity to facilitate that quest while at the same time facilitating the client's parallel quest. The darkness and horrors of the current world appear to reflect a deficiency of wisdom (perhaps we could call it existential ignorance) in much of humanity. Every client we help acquire more wisdom is a contribution to the remediation of that collective deficiency.

The core element of wisdom deficiency (I am struggling here to refrain from naming it "wisdom deficiency syndrome") is the lack of awareness that our sense of being separate from other humans (and all of life) is a very dangerous delusion. We might think of narcissism and psychopathy as merely being exaggerations of a normal sense of ourselves as fundamentally separate from others. However, it seems to me that all the religions and spiritual traditions of the world tell us that we are not fundamentally separate. Perhaps this is why they are often lumped together as "wisdom traditions."

It appears that modern psychotherapy is moving from reinforcing the delusion of separateness, under the banner of building ego strength and a strong sense of self, to challenging its actual validity. Jung (1916, 1953) contributed greatly to this challenge with the concept of the collective unconscious. Near the end of Jung's life Albert Hofmann planted a seed in modern civilizations for the further explorations of this challenge to the validity of the separate self when he discovered LSD. It soon became known as a valuable adjunct to psychotherapy because it seemed to facilitate access to the personal unconscious. However, it quickly became clear that LSD opened up something larger than the personal unconscious, perhaps called the collective unconscious or the transcendental realms, that was in direct conflict with the concept of a separate self. As work with LSD and similar medicines evolved, the dissolution of the ego became a specific intention of this work. Psychological preparations were made prior to the ingestion of the medicine to help facilitate this dissolution. Psychologists and philosophers might debate whether the dissolution of the ego is a temporary suspension of an existential truth of our fundamental separateness (i.e., a delusion) or if it is the realization of the deeper truth that the idea of a separate ego is a delusion. It seems that the positive effects of psychedelic-assisted psychotherapy last longer when patients who have experienced such transcendence of the self or ego remind themselves that they had that experience and that it was real.

The use of psychedelics has been growing exponentially over the last decade or two. Some has occurred in formal research settings such as medical schools and universities, where it is usually viewed as an adjunct to traditional symptom-focused psychotherapy. However, the vast majority has been taking place in a burgeoning underground movement that focuses more on the pursuit of life-changing transcendental experiences than on reducing symptoms like anxiety and depression.

This underground movement gives me great hope. To the extent that it is helping many people have experiences of themselves as being intrinsically part of all of humanity and even part of all of life, it makes it harder for these people to do things that are injurious to other humans or to the rest of the life forms on the planet. In fact it moves them in the direction of the hippie bumper sticker of the late '60s: "Peace and Love." The fact that there are increasing numbers of people who have had such deeply transformative experiences also implies that there are more opportunities for these people to gather with each other and reinforce the idea that these experiences are real, rather than just trippy fantasies. To have amnesia for the fact that spiritual experiences even occurred is also common—and led me many years ago to print up a batch of my own wise-guy bumper stickers that said "FORGET AMNESIA!"

It appears to me that the world as we know it is in great danger as a result of the human tendency to remain ignorant of, or amnesic for, the experiences that can lead to wisdom. The rise of dictatorships, ecological disaster, genocide, religious persecution, increasing wealth disparity, racism, and the like all depend on things like malignant othering syndrome (Rhead, 2021) and wealth acquisition and hoarding addictive disorder (Rhead and Clark 2019). While these conditions may be viewed as forms of individual psychopathology in need of individual psychotherapeutic healing, they can also be seen as collective forms of psychopathology in need of collective healing. I believe that the underlying psychopathology in either case can best be viewed in terms of the absence of, or amnesia for, wisdom. While radical interventions like 500 mcg of LSD or 30 days of restricted diet in a silent meditation retreat can help us acquire and retain wisdom, so can a weekly psychotherapy session with a therapist who sees increasing wisdom as their own goal. ▼

References

Hofmann, A., & Ott, J. (1980). *LSD, my problem child.* New York: McGraw-Hill.

Jung, C. G. (1953). *Collected Works,* Volume 7, "The structure of the unconscious" (1916), # 437-507, pp. 263-292.

Rhead, J. (2021). Malignant othering syndrome: Causes, consequences, treatment, and prevention. *Voices: The Art and Science of Psychotherapy, 57*(2), 33-39.

Rhead, J. & Clark, M. (2019). Wealth acquisition and hoarding addictive disorder. *Explore: The Journal of Science and Healing, 15*(1), 65-68.

ATARAXIA

J Grant

Renewal comes now
along with the flowers and sweet smells of sensual pleasures.

After the darkness and painful sufferings,
what happened was
Unexpected.
Serendipitous.

Searching for delight and gratification,
leaping toward adventure,

which had flirted with me

from youth to winnowing wisdom;

ready to move into the realm of forbidden fruit,

eager to taste the sweet nectar.
What happened
as I dared to be bold,
was a cascade of revelation--
a path to serenity,

leading me to the power of love
and my true identity.

Drawing Resilience From Our Pets

Kay Loveland, PhD

Asheville, North Carolina
kayloveland1@aol.com

The COVID pandemic has significantly impacted our lives. Routines are disrupted, contact with friends and family more limited, interactions with clients often on Zoom, and pleasurable, social activities such as attending movies or eating out at a restaurant greatly restricted. The constant possibility of contagion keeps us, at least most of us, facing a more enclosed life, and the frustration and sense of deprivation grows as time extends without an end in sight. So where can we turn for contact, unconditional love, and distraction? For many of us the answer is right in front of us, on our laps, licking our noses, sleeping on the couch, or munching hay in the barn. Our beloved animals are there, wanting to give us love and attention and demanding from us interaction, play, affection, and food!

Numerous studies have shown that contact with pets helps to reduce stress and anxiety, particularly in high-stress situations. In addition, pets can help people deal with social isolation and loneliness. They can motivate us to exercise even when we want to stay in bed, and they can even increase serotonin and dopamine levels in humans and decrease the risk of high blood pressure or heart attacks.

In my own life, I have experienced the positive effect of animals on myself and family members and have also witnessed the impact on my clients, foster children, patients in the hospital, and inmates in our local jail and prison, where I visited with my two therapy dogs. Several years ago, I participated in trauma resiliency model (TRM) training and Resources for Resilience. One resiliency skill, called resourcing, asks that the participant think of an event, a person or place, or something about themselves that triggers positive memories, then focus on the sensations in the body triggered by that detailed positive memory. By far, the most popular resource was a memory of an interaction with a favorite animal.

Relying on this knowledge, I developed a program that incorporated resiliency training and the participation of service dogs, and eventually opened Camp Hope Unleashed for veterans with severe PTSD. The veterans learned various skills to deal with their triggers, and the dogs learned to be of assistance. For example, when a veteran awoke with nightmares and terrors, the service dog was trained to climb on his or her chest to provide safety and pressure, and the veteran was taught to focus in on the sensations of pressure and warmth and safety. The camp also included techniques for the veterans to learn to help the dogs stay happy and resilient, such as Tellington TTouch and using music especially formulated to sooth dogs.

My clients often ask about my two dogs, as at least one had always been in the in-person sessions providing safe contact and unconditional love. Often, they make a guest appearance on the Zoom sessions, and, in turn, my clients share their dogs, cats, gerbils, and even snakes. Although I do not love Zoom, meeting the extended family of my clients is lovely, and on several occasions, teaching my clients to focus in on positive sensations as they pet their animals has been a good adjunct to reducing anxiety or stress.

Since my own dogs have been such help to me during the pandemic and prolonged health challenges, my thought was to write an article for Voices, but I was also very interested to learn more about other therapists and their animals during the pandemic. As expected, I was not the only one grateful for the animal-human connection. Don Murphy writes about his rescue pup, Annie, "an endearing distraction." Annie Prescott describes life and circadian rhythm with two dogs, one cat, four birds, and four horses. Barbara Sachs, Stephanie Ezust, and Giuliana Reed pay tribute to beloved pets that passed away during the pandemic. And Bradley Lake gives partial credit to dogs for helping him to find just the right partner and build a family. In the articles that follow, we share our stories of comfort, resilience, and hope drawn from the connection with our pets during difficult times. ▼

Kay Loveland

Kay Loveland, PhD, is a clinical psychologist from Asheville, North Carolina, and a long- time member of the American Academy of Psychotherapists. She has a particular interest in the animal-human bond and was co-founder of Camp Hope Unleashed for veterans with PTSD and their service dogs and director of Camp Unleashed, for other people and their dogs, for many years. In addition, she has written articles and presented workshops on animal-assisted psychotherapy. She has been fortunate to be part of several Pet Therapy teams with her well-loved goldendoodles.
kayloveland1@aol.com

Paws On My Heart

For the past few years, my life has been dominated by two significant health crises: the COVID pandemic that permeates all our lives and my own personal health crisis caused by the improper withdrawal from a medication prescribed for migraine prevention. The withdrawal and the subsequent medical errors involved in the treatment of it have left me with relentless debilitating symptoms. Both challenges greatly impact my life, and my resilience and fortitude are tested on a daily basis. Without the support of my significant other, Patrick, and my friends, my journey would be even more isolated and difficult. Several of these friends happen to be of the canine variety. My day-to-day existence has been immensely enhanced by their love, playfulness, and ability to give great cuddles.

At the beginning of my health crisis, in September of 2019, I had two wonderful dogs. Rowan, a standard goldendoodle, loved to cuddle on the couch and in the bed, enjoyed working as a therapy dog in my office, and for years visited children in the local hospital. She was also an integral part of our trauma resiliency program at the local jail. Her little buddy, Juniper, is a delightful, impish, and incredibly smart mini goldendoodle who likes to run the household and keep everyone on time. As my health deteriorated, they were there with me, offering comfort, company, distraction, and love.

Unfortunately, by January of 2020, my physical and mental health was fragile from various medical and pharmacologic interventions, each of which only seemed to increase symptoms and complications. On the Internet, I discovered a center in Arizona that promised to use healthy techniques and supplements to restore brain and body functioning. Out of desperation, after speaking with the staff, I decided to participate in the program.

Flying out to the center was a challenge, but I made the trip and arrived at what seemed to be a lovely facility with healthy food, alternative care such as acupuncture, massage, and sauna, and a doctor who claimed to be well-versed in tapering medications. Over time I realized that the program was not offering what was promised, but by then I was too ill to travel back to Asheville.

Three weeks into the program I received a call from Patrick who informed me that Rowan had terminal cancer. My sweet Rowan whom I had rescued from the ocean in wintery 55-degree water; Rowan who was the only bucket list item of my departed husband, Bruce; Rowan who helped me deal with his passing. I was devastated that she might die before I could return home, and the thought of her suffering without me was inconceivable. She had been placed on oral chemotherapy and made some progress, but the vet was clear that her time was limited. He said that a long road trip would not be a problem and that the chances were good that she would not live more than a few more months. Patrick decided that he would drive from Asheville to Arizona with both dogs so that Rowan and I would have a chance to say good-bye. When he shared his plans, my heart flooded with love for him and for them, and I felt a light amidst all of the darkness that I had been experiencing.

The three of them arrived at the facility on a warm February afternoon. Rowan came in the gate and spied me sitting on a rock in the courtyard. She ran top speed towards me, red curls flying. All 65 pounds of doodle launched exuberantly into my lap, and I held on to her like a dying person holds on to a life preserver. My tears started to flow, and Juni also crawled into my lap for snuggles. Patrick put his arms around me, and we

both cried from the joy of seeing each other and the sadness of Rowan's imminent death. I have rarely felt so loved and so loving. We spent several days hanging out together, taking little walks, watching sunsets, and petting the dogs. The center allowed Rowan and Juni to visit with the other participants, and the atmosphere of the house changed with a definite increase in laughter and energy.

I talked to Rowan about my gratitude to her and all that she had given to so many people in her work as a therapy dog. I told her how much I loved her and how she had helped me deal with Bruce's death and my health problems. I assured her that we would not let her suffer. She understood my tone and love, if not the actual words, and gazed at me intently as I spoke to her. I asked her to hold on until I came home if she could, and when I finished talking she lay beside me and put her sweet head in my lap. Patrick and I discussed euthanasia and decided that if she was suffering too much we would put her down, and I would be with her by phone if that time came. Way too soon Patrick and the dogs had to leave for their long trip home. I was filled with ambivalence. Certainly I was filled with joy and happiness from the wonderful visit, but I was also very worried that I would never see Rowan again, and the problems of the center that had promised so much were beginning to be revealed.

Subsequent to Rowan and Juni's visit, the staff was kind enough to entertain my suggestion of adding pet therapy to the program. I contacted the local Pet Partners organization and soon a lovely golden retriever began visiting a few times a week. In addition, the therapist began to bring her dog to work, and this wonderful and sweet pup and I took many walks together or just had visits in my room. My time with these dogs helped me to deal with the long, difficult days and provided a wonderful distraction. Playing with a dog, throwing a ball, and giving tummy rubs are all things that lift the spirit and help healing. Unfortunately, the visits stopped in early March when the specter of COVID first appeared.

One of the new clients at the facility had a hacking cough, and I wondered if he might have the virus. No one was being screened or tested for COVID, staff or participants, so I isolated in my room as much as possible. I had received a 10-day intravenous treatment that was supposed to really help my heath, but instead it sent me into a downward spiral, so staying in my room was not a problem. By this time I realized that the program was not safe in a number of ways and that I needed to leave before COVID spread to everyone. In addition, the admissions process began to allow clients that had a history of acting out and some violence, and on several occasions police had to be called to deal with dangerous situations. Patrick flew out, and I met him at the airport in Phoenix, which was eerily empty. We were fortunate in that our flight to Charlotte was one of the only ones that had not been cancelled. The trip was grueling, but a wheelchair at the airport helped considerably. I could not wait to get home.

When I walked into my house two happy dogs greeted me with immense enthusiasm. Can you imagine if we greeted each other every day like our dogs greet us? Tails wagged, tongues licked at top speed, and voices lifted in howling joy! Rowan looked healthy and happy, and I was filled with relief. I sat on the floor and let them have their way with me. There is nothing quite like happy dog slobber!

We understood that Rowan's time was limited, and even though I was still having great difficulty, we planned for a week at the beach—both for my benefit and to give Rowan one last fling at her favorite place, Hilton Head Island. Fortunately, the beach

was not crowded, and we were well masked. We stayed on the beach or in the beach house. I could not walk far but watched the dogs frolic, chase each other, roll in the sand, and greet other dogs. This provided me with a sense of happiness and great joy and a much-needed distraction from health crises, personal and global. The sunsets were also an inspiration to stop long enough to notice beauty.

Soon after the beach trip, Rowan began to weaken, and one day she stopped eating. We consulted with the vet. After tests and bloodwork, the decision was clear. Rowan's time with us was ending. We called Four Paws Farewell, and the vet arrived at our home the next day. We were all masked, and Rowan was lying on a dog bed in our front yard as we petted and talked to her. Several neighbors came, masked, to stand vigil just outside the fence. The vet gave her two injections as I held her in my arms and told her that she was the best dog. She passed peacefully. I snipped some of her fur to keep, and the vet loaded her in her van and drove away. Rowan had stayed alive for 6 months longer than expected. Having her with me was a blessing, and losing her was heartbreak.

My difficult withdrawal from the medications continued, and I discovered that the process was going to last a few more years. Days ranged from intolerable to just making it, with constant nausea, weakness, fatigue, migraine headaches, and myriad other problems. I found some good medical help, but unfortunately, no shortcuts to health. I missed Rowan: her cuddles, her silly antics, her love. And I wasn't the only one. Juni was obviously depressed and became withdrawn, losing her exuberance and confidence. Patrick was grieving Rowan as well. After several discussions, we decided to add a puppy to the household. Perhaps this wasn't the best time to add a puppy, but Patrick had moved in with me, and we just decided to go for it! A few months later we added Jasper to our family. He is a red and white mini goldendoodle, full of exuberance and friendliness. We all were immediately in love, including Juni, who perked up and began playing with her brother with wild abandon. They played, cuddled, and ran together, and watching

them was more uplifting than any Saturday morning cartoon.

The COVID pandemic was in full swing by this time, and we were isolated from most friends and family. However, just downhill from my house is a large field and some woods, and on days when I felt very weak, I still made it a goal to take the dogs down to the field and throw the Chuck-it. Sometimes that was the only thing I accomplished, but on stronger days I was able to take the two dogs for a walk around the block. My need to take care of and enjoy time with them was enough of an incentive to get me out of bed or off the couch and added a small amount of exercise as well as some fun.

Neighbors became quite used to seeing the two dogs on our walks and called out greetings as we passed. One family with three girls asked if they could play with the dogs if they wore masks and we kept a distance, so I put the dogs on 6-ft leashes and taught the girls some of the basic obedience commands to use with Jasper and Juni. They all became very attached to each other, and the parents have decided that the girls had so much fun that they were ready for their own dog! We continue to visit, and I look forward to the interactions with the girls who were so caring and accepting of a rather rambunctious puppy. The time together always uplifts my spirits.

Perhaps the most hope and help during this challenging time has come from my neighbor across the field and her own goldendoodle, Emily. Peggy and I have been friends since we were young psychologists in Atlanta. Somehow, we both ended up in in Asheville, and we live less than a block from each other. Recently, Emily suffered from either a stroke or disease process that left her hind legs paralyzed. Peggy was faced with the possibility of losing her. She was devastated, as Emily had been her constant companion during COVID, and made the decision to give it 2 weeks to see if she improved. Against all odds, in a few days Emily began to move her legs, then stand, then walk with assistance and a sling. Now she is fully mobile and almost back to her old self. The joy we felt when Emily began to walk, and then to run, was uplifting and a great example for me that healing is possible.

Almost every day, Peggy and Emily either come over to my house to visit, or I walk over to theirs with one or both of my dogs. Sometimes the walk to her house can be quite taxing, but making the effort is satisfying and important. Once there, we settle on her newly enclosed back porch/bedroom with huge picture windows. Peggy and Emily relax on the bed, and I chill out on the futon with Jasper and Juni, their warm little dog bodies cuddled up to my back. We listen to music or ask Alexa to read us a story. For whatever reason, the first time we asked her for a story, she started on *The Tales of Beatrix Potter*, and thus began our back porch tradition: one short silly story a day about rabbits or mice, two relaxed humans, and our very chill dogs. This time of relaxation and comfort has quickly become my favorite time of the day. Just imagine, if you can, the scene: two good friends totally relaxing with their sweet dogs, looking out to the trees and watching the silly squirrels play tag round and round the tree trunk, spotting the various types of birds preparing for colder weather, then closing eyes and forgetting everything else but the comfort of the friendships, human and canine.

I don't know how much longer either the pandemic or my own health struggle will last. Neither has an end in sight, so what I can attempt is to make the best of the better days, fill my life with friendship and love, and snuggle with my best four-legged buddies, who are unaware of either intrusion and approach each day with exuberance acting as if I am almost as wonderful as scraps accidentally dropped on the floor. ▼

Small Package, Big Impact

Don Murphy, PhD

Decatur, Georgia
doncm38@gmail.com

Our last boxer, Olivia, died 15 years ago, and since her death we had been saying to each other, Barbara and I, that our frequent travel made it too difficult to have a pet. Moreover, my cousin Mark, who had been our trusted pet sitter for years, had the audacity to up and move away for a new lease on his own life.

And then the pandemic descended. Our conversation re-surfaced, and we decided to go for it. Being of a certain age now, we felt that a large dog would not be best for us, nor would having the stress of a puppy. So, we spread the word that we were looking for a small, hypoallergenic, female dog who was house and crate trained, obedient, cuddly, at least a year old, etc. This list of conditions led one of our friends to laughingly say to us that it was as if we were asking for a bootleg plumber who only worked on Tuesdays from 3:00-5:00, only for women, and had a barely dependable truck!

Our friend, however, did not know about the persistence of our granddaughter, Emma, who has had, from early childhood, the reputation as the family "finder." Whatever was lost. Emma was able to locate it. She employed that same instinct in search of our pet. For a year Emma sent us, almost daily, photos of dogs she had found, always the right size, etc., but often too far away. Those she discovered nearby would be taken by the time we had inquired of them. That was true until Annie. Emma sent us a photo of this precious white shaggy mutt who had just been brought into a nearby shelter, and we sped there immediately.

She looked awful. Clearly, she had been on the street for some time, given her thick, dirty, and matted coat, and we did not know until having her at home for a while whether or not she met our stringent conditions. We bathed her at the shelter and brought her home a couple of days later. She soon checked all the boxes.

We chose to name our new love Annie, after the Irish lass Annie Moore, who was the first immigrant to step onto Ellis Island back in the day. We were amazed at how quickly she began responding to her new name, although it must have been initially disconcerting. She adapted quickly to her new home and to us. Right away she slept through the night and was quick to signal us when she needed to go out during the day. Moreover, she loves physical contact, often jumping up into the chair with either of us. In other words, she had us at hello!

As with most folks, the pandemic has put us into occasional doldrums, and our family experienced an additional trauma in the form of a serious accident of our oldest daughter, Deana. A scooter mishap in Rome, Italy, just before Thanksgiving resulted in a badly broken tibia plate. What followed was an absolute nightmare: 15 days in a Rome hospital, mounting anxiety at our being so far away from her, and botched surgery that had to be redone when she came home. For several reasons, we were unable to go to Italy to be with her, an almost unbearable experience.

During this anxious time, Annie has been an endearing distraction. Not only are we calmed by just holding her, but her playfulness lifts our spirits. One of our favorite activities is walking her in the local cemetery a block from our home. The setting is beautiful with rolling hills, lots of trees, a creek, and a couple of clear meadows. If no one else is there when we take Annie, we ignore the leash law and turn her loose. Immediately she starts running in wide circles around us, and just as immediately our spirits lift.

So, with the love and determination of Emma, hope has blessed us in the engaging, energetic, and loving presence of Annie: small package, big impact for sure. ▾

You don't need to be a heroin addict or a performance artist to experience extremity. You just have to love someone.

—Nick Hornsby, *How to Be Good*

The very least you can do in your life is figure out what you hope for. And the most you can do is live inside that hope. Not admire it from a distance but live right in it, under its roof.

—Barbara Kingsolver, *Animal Dreams*

Annie Prescott

ANNIE PRESCOTT, PhD, CCS, CAC II, CCJTS, has been a clinician since 1979. Being raised with horses and dogs led to an early vision of wanting to help others heal using the power of being in relationship with animals. She pursued her doctorate in clinical psychology with a specialty in psychoneuroimmunology. Dr. Prescott's private psychotherapy practice provides holistic treatment options for adults, adolescents, and children with addictive and mental disorders as a result of trauma exposure. In her free time, she enjoys horseback riding, camping, travelling, exercising, and daily meditation.
prescottannie77@gmail.com

Animal Connection During the COVID-19 Pandemic

ANIMALS ARE DRIVEN AND LIVE BY THEIR CIRCADIAN RHYTHMS. They experience an innate knowledge of getting their basic needs met through eating, sleep, exercise, play, and stillness. This natural, internal state repeats itself every 24 hours. Animals seek connection and thrive best when they have companions of their own species. However, animals respond well to inter-species connection also, especially with humans. Owning two dogs, a cat, four birds, and four horses has kept me on schedule with my own circadian rhythm of self-care during this COVID-19 pandemic, over the last 2 years. Caring for animals gives me a sense of purpose and feeling that I am making a small difference in the world, my animals' world. We all need to feel important and a sense of significance. Animals provide unconditional acceptance and love. They do not care how we look or how we feel. Reciprocally, we depend on each other.

In February 2020, I was recovering from a double cervical discectomy and fusion of C-3 and C-4. This was the most difficult physical challenge I have experienced in my entire life. Without the surgery, I was informed that I would eventually become paralyzed. I am a high energy, physically active woman, and could not imagine being restricted. I felt fear, considering the high-risk procedure and potential consequences. I knew that my natural care-giving nature would be halted in exchange for my immediate need to receive care from others during my rehabilitation. But I chose to undergo the surgery. I was not fully informed about the challenges of my recovery. Less than 24 hours after the surgery, I was discharged to my home. Despite my spouse's loving care, I needed full-time nursing support, which I discovered after a week of suf-

fering. Feeling so helpless and needy was terrifying. Frequently, unable to sleep, I cried out in desperation with anger and prayers for relief. My two dogs slept near me, at times waking me up to alert me that I needed pain medication. Their intuitive, empathic sense and unconditional loving affection brought me moments of comfort. The hardest part of this journey was patiently waiting the suggested 6 months to ride my horses again. I was determined to recover as quickly as possible. Fortunately, living with my horses on my horse farm, I could walk short distances outdoors and feel comfort hearing the horses' loving nickers. Touching and caressing these great creatures and feeling their strong supportive presence gave me more motivation and hope. With each passing day, I felt my growing strength return and my pain decrease. Four months after my surgery, I took my first ride again. It was one of the happiest days of my life.

During this same time, the world began to shut down because of the highly contagious COVID-19 virus leading to more and more deaths. Quarantine and isolation from our friends and family members became our new normal. The daily media reports escalated people's anxiety. The necessary protective pulling in and being inside our homes led to loneliness. Staying connected to others became more challenging. Physical touch between our loved ones, other than the ones we lived with, was halted. However I was blessed to find an escape and solace from being with my animal family.

Having to arise early each morning to feed my animals provides routine, structure, and discipline. Hearing the morning barking alerts and motivates me to arise from my slumber to let my dogs outside, make my first cup of strong coffee, and enjoy the aroma. My mouth waters with anticipation of the first sip and the quiet time as the dogs and cat eat their breakfast. Listening to the birds chirping and singing greets me as my body,

mind, and sprit awaken. I bundle up because of the winter chill before going out to feed my beloved horses. I witness my breath exhalation with a crystallized condensation of cool air and head to the barn nearby. The pastures are frosted and twinkle in the moonlight sky. The dawn, before the sun rises, is a very precious time for me. As I enter the tack room, the aroma fills the area with leather-soaked bridles and saddles along with horsehair-filled saddle blankets. As I prepare the horse feed, I breathe in the oats and grain being poured into their individual buckets. I notice that some of the buckets have names crossed out from previous horses raised here at our Oakhill farm. I smile with the memory of each beloved horse etched in my mind and held in my heart, each one having taught me various lessons during many stages of my life. As I enter my horse family's stalls, I hear their whinnies greeting me, and I see their anticipation and excitement as I pour their feed into their troughs. Listening to their first few bites of feed, I smile at their enthusiastic, rhythmic munching. I know they are being nurtured by not only nutrients from the feed but also my loving intention with caring routines.

This mirrors my own self-care routine as I find either my sacred indoor or outdoor spaces to enjoy my daily meditation, focusing on my prayers of gratitude and intentional healing. It is a time of connection with my animals and my inner self. My slow, rhythmic stretching and breathing practice includes yoga, tai chi, qigong, and tapping, to further awaken my entire being. Journaling is also a part of my self-care ritual. Having my two dogs, Lady and Mr. Peabody, accompanying me in my meditation room, one on either side of my meditation postures, I rhythmically stroke their soft fur. I understand that rhythm helps to activate the relaxation response in the brain and body, further deepening my pleasant state of being. My dogs are a source of comfort and connection, and it feels reciprocal. Their soulful looks into my eyes are loving and unconditional. When I speak directly to them, they cock their heads with curiosity and knowing. A soft paw on my foot alerts me to notice them as they communicate their needs, or it just validates that they want to be seen.

Max, my 3-year-old cat, is curled up in a blanketed chair. He reminds me that rest and stillness are crucial for balance in my sometimes overly active lifestyle. Being playful with simple objects or the other animals provides brief periods of entertainment. A slow blink of Max's eyes reassures me of his love and affection as I slowly blink back with reciprocal confirmation. His occasional flopping down in my path reminds me to take the time to rub his belly and give him a quick body massage. He purrs with delight. I believe we should all receive a spontaneous belly rub, don't you?

The four birds, Sherman, Pepi, Birdie, and Spirit Bird, sing me various greetings as they also arise with the sun glowing through the French doors into their cage. It is lovely to hear. Observing the birds' self-preening and beak-kissing interactions reveals their own social desires.

During this 2-year pandemic period, I changed my horse herd. I sold one horse and purchased another, on the same day! This is highly unusual. An older woman was looking to purchase a safe, well-trained horse, and another person was selling a well-mannered horse to a good home. They were the same Rocky Mountain breed that I have come to love for their sound mind and desires to connect with humans. This arrangement fell into place with synchronicity. Bringing Buddy Mack home to acclimate to his new home took strategy and patience. I have two other mares, Bella and Xena Warrior Princess, and another gelding named Kaydon. They have been a part of my herd family for many years. I chose to place Buddy Mack with Xena, as Bella and Kaydon have always been "peas and carrots" companions, great together.

Xena and Buddy Mack bonded quickly as they rode together in the trailer back to Oakhill, after purchasing him. Initially the pairs were separated into different pastures as they became familiar with each other. In the evenings, the horses are kept in the stables. Their stalls are adjacent to each other so that they can socialize. The herd quickly accepted Buddy Mack as they are able to sniff noses in an encircled fashion. I find myself in horse heaven as I stand in the middle of this circle as each horse nuzzles me and attempts to get my attention to give them loving touches. I adore the connection between us, as I lean into their nostrils, breathing into their warm exhalation, as we exchange our life force and mutual affection.

It has only been recently that the herd joined together as one. There is a hierarchical positioning within a herd. With geldings (male horses), there is usually a power struggle in establishing who is the herd leader. Kaydon has been the lookout leader and protector horse for many years. Bella is the head mare. Xena joined the herd almost 3 years ago, so she has been the lowest horse on the totem pole. Buddy Mack had been in a pasture alone for some time before coming to Oakhill. He was not fed grain, because of getting too much pastureland. Once he arrived, he was anxious during feeding times, anticipating being fed. He would tap dance and rear up a bit while making whining sounds, begging to be fed. Speaking to him calmly by saying "easy" or "settle" would ease his impatience until I walked to his bucket to fill it with feed. Slowly increasing his feed and hay, Buddy Mack began to calm himself more easily as he trusted he would be regularly fed.

Watching a new horse be accepted into a new herd reminds me of what it can be like

for us, for me, coming into a new group or community: for example, joining the American Academy of Psychotherapists (AAP) circle. Tentative, unsure, nervous, somewhat mistrusting, but also hungry for connection, acceptance, belonging, and nurturing—sometimes experiencing these competing emotions and desires simultaneously. Quietly observing the group mores, hierarchal structure, and activities, I might initially feel hesitant and anxious to speak out in the group, even while yearning for that connection and inclusion. Eventually, this leads to testing the waters with more disclosures. Sometimes we feel bitten on the flank, kicked, or rejected from the group. Sometimes we feel nuzzled and stroked and protected by the reactions we receive from others. Hopefully, we survive the initial discomfort, and we find our place.

Walking outdoors, my horse herd encircles me with curiosity and anticipation of receiving rhythmic, nurturing strokes upon their velvety, furry winter coats. I offer big hugs around their necks as well as yummy treats now and then. I feel connected, and my body immediately relaxes as I entrain to their relaxed, mindful presence. I quickly become acutely aware, awake, and mindfully present.

I have felt that way in Academy events also and have missed my connection with my AAP family during this pandemic separation. I look forward to future face-to-face meetings again. I anticipate arriving with open arms, a wide smile, and playful enthusiasm. I will feel like I am held, protected, and encircled in love, once again. Just like Buddy Mack must be feeling a sense of belonging in his new horse family, accepted and loved. ▼

Barbara Sachs, LPC

Atlanta, Georgia
bysachs@yahoo.com

My Dog Talked and I Listened:
Lessons from the Pandemic

It was Scooter, my cockapoo rescue, who helped me through the beginnings of the COVID pandemic. Even though he is gone now, he helps me still. That is the nature of a deep relationship; it is not over even after a life ends.

I adopted Scooter when he was 2, as I tried to manage my depression resulting from an orthopedic surgery. He and his brother had been surrendered to a vet with instruction from the owner to "just put them down. They are too much trouble." They had been abused and their care neglected. His brother died of Parvo, and Scooter barely survived. We seemed a perfect fit.

When I brought Scooter home, he hid from me under the bed. He was so traumatized by life that one day he tried to jump through a closed window when my husband raised his voice. It took over a month of work for me to be able to pet him; I lay on the floor, flat on my back, with my arms outstretched and a treat inches away from my fingers. Over time, I moved the treats closer and closer until I was able to gently touch, then finally pet him.

I learned patience, kindness, and consistency. Over time, I earned his trust and love. The memory I hold on to the tightest is that of Scooter getting on the couch next to me and from there into my lap. He would find the perfect spot on my cheek and give me doggie kisses, getting more and more insistent, until we were wrestling on the floor in playful abandon. How can a person respond to trust and love, other than with joy?

Scooter was my teacher. He taught me the importance of trusting others and that only by creating ties with others can I connect with myself. Treating myself with the same patience, curiosity, and kindness with which I strive to treat others helps me to remain upright in a world that can feel both abusive and neglectful. Scooter exemplified resilience. He taught me to live therapy, not just practice it.

In Memoriam: Scooter 2002—2020

Stephanie Ezust

STEPHANIE EZUST, PhD, a psychologist in Decatur, Georgia, has been working as a psychotherapist since 1976. She currently works with trauma survivors, and increasingly with people around issues of ageing, illness, and dying. She lives with two rescue Siamese kittens who are about to celebrate their first birthday. She enjoys music (always hoping to reclaim that piano in the living room), movies, and books, as well as dancing, walking, and hiking, and most importantly, connecting with friends and family.
drezust@comcast.net

Bodhi and Lily

I HAVE LOVED AND LIVED WITH ANIMALS ALL MY LIFE. I grew up with a dog and an outdoor cat, and when I moved into my first apartment in college I got a Siamese cat, the first in a long line of Siamese cats. I did not come back to dogs until a long time later, when I was living with a man who worked as a postal carrier. When we moved in together, he immediately got a golden retriever puppy, but she was his dog. Some years later, he found a stray dog who had been hanging around a factory on his route for some time. He brought the dog home. We agreed that we would care for the starving dog over the weekend and take him to a vet on the Monday to have them find a home for him. However, this dog, who seemed to be made of spare parts, and who turned out to have every parasite known to dog, including heartworms, did worm his way into my heart, and of course we ended up keeping him. I named him Papageno, because like the bird catcher in *The Magic Flute*, he came out of the woods, no one knew who his parents were, his tail was feathered, and when he first arrived he did not bark (in the opera, Papageno, who talked too much, irritated the Queen of the Night so much that she placed a padlock on his mouth, and there it stayed until he had gone through the necessary rites of passage). We nursed Papageno through the heartworms and the other parasites, and he eventually got his bark back: He would "read the news" to the neighborhood every morning once he recovered. The vet estimated that he was about 6 when he came to us, and he lived for 6 more

years, bringing me much joy. I came up with the phrase "joy bubbles," the sensation I felt in my heart watching him enthusiastically chasing squirrels in the park, as I remembered how close to death he had been when he first came to me.

But this article is about Bodhi. I've told you about Papageno, the first of many rescue dogs in my life, because I want you to know that I've never gone looking for a dog; they have always found me. I had two large dogs, Rumi and Sadie, both of whom lived to be about 16. Because they were large dogs, and because by then I was living alone, it was really difficult to lift them by myself as they aged and became unable to get up on their own. So I would need to get friends to come and help me lift them when that was necessary. When they died, I decided that I would never again have a dog that I could not pick up myself. I was also clear that I wanted my next dog to be a therapy dog. I did some research and decided that I wanted a cockapoo. I checked rescue sites, and if I had wanted to go to Arizona, there was a lovely cockapoo puppy available immediately, but I live in Atlanta, and that was not practical. Then I remembered that I had never gone looking for a dog; they had all come to me. So I put a message out to the universe with an image of the dog I was looking for. Three days later my longest-standing client came to me and said, "We have a litter of cockapoo puppies. Would you like one?" Under most circumstances this would be totally inappropriate, with all the boundary and ethical issues that could arise, but the timing was uncanny and I knew I needed to pay attention. I consulted with a member of the American Academy of Psychotherapists ethics committee and processed the offer up and down with my client. After what felt like due diligence, I decided to accept the gift. On Christmas Eve, 2010, I met my client in a parking lot half way between where she lived and where I lived, and she placed this adorable little bundle of joy in my arms. I also met his father, the cocker spaniel in the mix, who had come to see his son off.

It took about a year, I think, before Bodhi was ready to be with me in the consulting room. He was so smart that he quickly learned the commands that most good dogs learn. But I did not teach him his therapy instincts. These were his alone. You might know that the word "Bodhi" is an abbreviation for "Bodhisattva," which in Buddhist teachings is an enlightened being who has remained incarnate in order to help others grow towards enlightenment. I had no idea when I chose this name for him how appropriate it would be. When Bodhi first came to me, I had two Siamese cats (remember the line of cats who have been with me since college?). They were 10 years old when he arrived, and it had been a while since they had lived with a dog. They were not amused. Ali, the male cat, hissed and swiped at him. Bodhi had never seen a cat before, and he thought it was a game, so he swiped back, and the game was on. Lily, the female cat, was about a third bigger than Ali, who had been the runt of their litter, and she bullied him constantly. But the first hint that something magical was afoot came when Bodhi brought harmony into our home. Lily stopped bullying Ali, and all three got along beautifully. Ali died a few years later, but Lily lived to be just over 20 years old, and Bodhi and Lily were cuddle buddies.

Once Bodhi started accompanying me to work, he got the hang of his job almost immediately. He had a bed in my office, and he would start the session from there. As each client walked in the door, the part that I definitely did not teach him came into play: He would do a sort of assessment of what they needed that day. If they did not want him involved, he would stay on his bed. If they needed him exuberant and affectionate, he

would provide that. If they needed comfort and gentleness, he was there for them. If a client began to cry, he would come over and sit at their feet, looking up at them. If they indicated that he was welcome, he would jump up into their lap. I work with many trauma survivors, and when Bodhi would sit in a client's lap, they would stroke his silky fur and often begin to talk, saying things they had never before told anyone. The client who gave me Bodhi had a diagnosis of dissociative identity disorder (DID), and Bodhi was instrumental in helping her to integrate over the years. She would sit with him in her lap, and she would then be able to process from each of her parts, with Bodhi providing the anchor that allowed her to remain present as she slowly began to integrate those dissociated parts.

Four years ago I received a diagnosis of breast cancer. About 6 months earlier, Lily was diagnosed with renal failure, and she became pretty ill, seemingly ready to die. However, she apparently changed her mind, and I am convinced that she wanted to be with me through my treatment. I don't know how I would have navigated that difficult time if Bodhi and Lily had not been there for me. When I recovered from the treatment, I thought she might go; she was receiving subcutaneous fluids two and three times a week. But she held on. And then the pandemic hit. Again, having these two companions with me through the lockdown was lifesaving for me. Bodhi didn't do very well on the computer, so he was a vital element missing from my Zoom sessions with clients. Lily, however, who had never been to my office, did connect with clients during some of the virtual sessions, although it was usually just to greet them.

In May 2021, Lily indicated that she was reaching the end of her time with us, and I had her euthanized in my home with Bodhi and my closest friend there to witness.

Bodhi and I both grieved this loss deeply. I had lived with Lily longer than any other being. She was 20 years and 3 weeks old.

Last July I went back to seeing clients in person, with a few remaining virtual, but most coming in person, with strict guidelines for vaccine and masks in place. Unfortunately, though, the Delta variant soon showed up, and I eventually went back to all virtual sessions. Sometime during the summer Bodhi began coughing, and eventually he was diagnosed with metastatic lung cancer. In Chinese medicine, the lungs are associated with grief, and I truly believe that he was missing Lily. I spoke with an animal communicator the day he received the diagnosis, and she told me that Bodhi was ready to die. She said that he and I have been together many times before and that we will be together again, serving people and other beings. This gave me a lot of comfort. I assured him that I wanted him to leave when he was ready and not to worry about me. On October 27th the same lovely vet came to my home to euthanize him, again with my close friend, Barbara, there to support and witness. Bodhi was settled in the living room when the vet arrived, so we decided to do the procedure there. It was quick, and Bodhi seemed to relax into it, going peacefully. My friend Barbara is a medical intuitive, and she told me that Bodhi's spirit left very quickly after the procedure, looking back at me before he left to see if I was ok. In my living room I have two paintings on facing walls. They are by an artist, Lee Lawson, whose paintings portray images of people she has said are part of an alternative universe. The figures look to me like Inuit women. The painting opposite the windows, over my piano, is of a woman holding a pottery jar. After the vet left, taking Bodhi's body with her, Barbara and I were standing in the living room, and suddenly Barbara said to me, "Look, Steffi!" She pointed to the painting of the woman holding the jar: Over the woman's heart there were two rainbows. There are no prisms in that room, and I have no idea where the rainbows came from, but both of us were sure that was Bodhi. A few hours later, after we had come back from getting some lunch, I was sitting at my dining room table, talking on the phone, making arrangements for Bodhi's cremation, and looking out the window into my back yard. There is a small addition on the back of my house that has a pitched roof, and I could see a corner of the roof from where I was sitting. As I sat there, a mourning dove flew to the corner of the roof and settled there, looking in the window at me. I called Barbara to come and see, and the dove seemed to make sure we both had seen her (I think it was a her), and then she flew away. I think those two events were both messages from Bodhi, and both gave me great comfort.

Over the next few weeks I had the additional job of sitting with my clients in their grief at his loss. Most people walked in asking almost immediately where he was, and I told them, and sometimes we cried together. I thought that it was diagnostic that a few clients never noticed (and still haven't after all this time) that he was not there, even after his bed was replaced with a plant on a stand. One client did not seem to notice Bodhi was not there, and we spent that session with him trying to access his feelings and his heart as his older brother faced life-threatening surgery. At the very end of the session, he looked at the spot where Bodhi's bed had been and asked where he was. When I told him that Bodhi had died the week before, he burst into tears, and we sat and cried together. Bodhi's final gift to him had been to help open his heart so that he could feel his sadness and fear about his brother's surgery.

I started this article telling you that I have loved and lived with animals all my life, but Bodhi was a special being, and I cherish the 11 years we had together. He had the gift of inviting people to share his exuberance and joy in life. I was in a training group through the Academy with four other women over several years. All but one of us are animal lovers. The fifth woman was definitely not a dog lover, and she reluctantly agreed that Bodhi could join us for one of our retreats. By the end of the 5 days he had seduced her, and she has shared my grief at this tremendous loss. Bodhi embodied joy, giving meaning to his name, an enlightened being whose purpose was to help other beings grow towards enlightenment. The theme for this issue of *Voices* is hope, and knowing that there are beings like Bodhi walking the planet offers me a profound source of hope. ▼

Ever wonder where you'd end up if you took your dog for a walk and never once pulled back on the leash?

—Robert Brault

The difference between friends and pets is that friends we allow into our company, pets we allow into our solitude.

—Robert Brault

I don't need that much to live – we don't need that much to have a wonderful life. I learned that from animals.

—Carrie Ann Inaba

Giuliana Reed, LICSW

Bethesda, Maryland
gvmreed@gmail.com

Scout

I should have known, when I glanced at her papers to notice her given name was Jade, that I might be in over my head. The name brought to mind a Chinese empress. This intuition proved remarkably accurate over the next few years. Blogs and articles encourage prospective dog owners to meet both of the pup's parents, but only her father seemed to be around when we went to fetch her. He appeared mild mannered enough, a cheerful sort of fellow. I ignored my nagging wondering about the mother. When she finally did make an appearance, bursting on the scene like a wild woman, in a combination of mayhem and chaos at her escape from wherever it was she had been, it was too late to turn back. Our Westie at the time, Cooper, understanding immediately the avuncular role he'd play for the rest of his life, had already fallen in love with her. We in turn were instantly enchanted by her quintessential Jack Russell looks: brown patch over one eye, brown feathery ears that gave her the grace of a ballerina in a tutu, and eyes that spelled mischief. We drove home through the autumn afternoon, the winding roads of the Shenandoah Valley causing her to throw up most of the way. She developed a terror of cars. I named her Scout, after the heroine in *To Kill a Mockingbird*. She grew courageous, smart, opinionated, and outspoken, and even overcame her fear of cars when I drove her at 2 mph to the dog park to let her run loose under Cooper's supervision. It only took one trip.

Scout died this last October at the age of 14. The vet came to the house to assist the transition. The three of us cried when it was all over. We even hugged; the pandemic be damned. Grieving her loss has been poignant and rich.

Scout marched to the beat of her own drum. By the time she was 2 she was running our household. She gave herself the job of household timekeeper, throughout the day telling us when it was time to get up, when to eat, when to play, when it was time to ride in the car or walk through the neighborhood, when she should be given treats (always), and when we should all go to bed. She even had opinions about which television shows we watched: nothing too loud or too violent. She didn't like rock and roll or harsh sounding music and would leave the room as if disgusted by our choices.

Scout was a skilled therapy dog, joyfully greeting clients at the door when they came for their sessions. Most of them loved her. As an empress, she would have rather not had our other dog, Mosby (a mild-mannered Westie, successor to Cooper), be a part of the family. This caused us to have to keep an eye on her during mealtimes lest she starve him to death with in-your-face growls that terrified him. She was determined to succeed. In her early adolescence, she concocted a plan to potty inside the house. She figured out that she could hide her BMs in the pattern of the Oriental rug in our living room, where these became quite literally invisible. She had many indoor places she might have used for this purpose, but the rug provided the deepest camouflage for her misdeeds. She was amazing that way, so mostly I had to admire her for her creativity and ingenuity. She appeared to be always thinking, calculating what her next move might be to get her way. More than anything however, she loved chasing tennis balls in the park. If we had thrown them as much as she would have liked, I'm pretty sure she would have died of a heart attack mid run. All the way back to the car from the park she would complain, "Throw the ball, throw the ball," jumping at our legs and running circles of seductive delight around us, her ears flapping in the breeze. She was relentless about the things she wanted and about her vision of how things should be. She was quite the pain in the ass sometimes. Somehow, this made us love her even more. When Scout wanted her dinner, she would come to me, give me a look until I said, "Oh, you want dinner? Coming right up." (She had me well trained.) She would then cross the breakfast room, jump in a chair (her chair), and gracefully cross her paws so that she could keep an eye on what I was doing. She waited for me to serve her. I kid you not. Every time. It made me feel like a servant, which probably was how she saw things. She got to demanding home-cooked food and would rather have starved than eat canned or dry. "Seriously, this is what you're trying to feed me? I am not eating this! I am not a dog!" With a disgusted look thrown in for good measure. There may even have been a "Go to hell!" in there. I'm certain she would have loved her own place at the dinner table.

Do I want her back? Of course I do. Do I cry and long for her sometimes? Yes. Yet grieving her has been different from any other grief I've experienced. I keep coming back to how rich it was to have been graced by her presence for 14 years, how lucky I was to watch her live her life to the fullest, by her own vision. I imagine Cooper greeting her at the Pearly Gates, where they've run off in a field together, like they did in that grassy field on the very first day they met. That's my girl, Scout, beloved companion and wise teacher. The quieter, slower pace of the pandemic created ample space to remember and reminisce, mostly with delight and rich tears. This has been a gift during these dark and turbulent times.

Bradley Lake

BRADLEY LAKE, LICSW, LCSW-C has been in private practice for over 30 years, providing psychotherapy to individuals, couples, and groups. Bradley is on the faculty of National Group Psychotherapy Institute (NGPI) at the Washington School of Psychiatry (WSP) as the Small Group Team Leader. He also works as a consultant for organizations and businesses, helping to identify areas of implicit bias and to bring about change towards greater awareness and equity inclusion. Bradley lives in Annapolis, Maryland, with his husband, two kids, and three dogs—all of which inspire him to know more about himself, the world in which he came from, and the one he currently resides in.

bradley_lake@yahoo.com

Two Plus Two Equals Four...and More

I WAS NEWLY SINGLE AND NOT WELL VERSED IN DATING. In fact, at the age of 40 I had never asked someone out for a date. Please note: This writing is not about digging deeper into the internal crevasses and meaning of that reveal; however, the reader can have a go at it. Rather, this story is about how and why I met my husband of 21 years with the help of two furry friends.

At the time, I was frustrated by my gentlemen suitors—handsome, well educated, and invested in dating me, yes. However, other characteristics that would draw me towards someone were often lacking—would he be curious about my journey to 40, or by my plan to pursue adopting a child, or by my chosen profession as a therapist, or my previous lives as a professional dancer and athlete. There was, I thought, a lot of good material to pepper me with questions and be curious about my internal world.

When not seeing clients, running, at the gym, or playing tennis, much of my time was spent with Jasper, my 12.5-lb Maltese. Maltese dogs were bred as chastity to royal women. They were seen as accessories for royalty. Jasper sat next to me in my therapy chair, usually snuggled up against my left leg during sessions with patients, for over a decade. Jasper had an astute awareness for psychopathology. Twice he disliked patients who were far from who they said they were and invited my skepticism only to discover criminal backgrounds—once leading me to call the FBI, and a long-standing crime case was solved.

Prior to this period in my life of being single, an 8-year relationship had ended. As is and should be true of any long relationship, with lives entangled, there was a great deal of pain—we hurt each other, and this informed anger and rage. At the time, I claimed the role of wounded party, and it was only over that next year of therapy that I realized my unconscious role. I wasn't behaviorally responsible for his affair, but I pushed away, poked, held resentments, and stayed in something that I wasn't willing to claim wasn't good or good enough for me.

We had two Maltese dogs, Jasper and Sal. In the mediation agreement, I asked for both dogs—revealing my edge. However, as I honored their relationship (perhaps more than mine) I considered that Jasper and Sal did not like one another. Perhaps they held greater clarity of their discordance with one another—a more conscious parallel process. I asked my ex if he could keep Sal, and I would take Jasper with me on to the next journey of my adult life. He agreed. As my ex and I went our separate ways, so did Jasper and Sal—the dyads shifted.

The many walks that Jasper and I took gave me great pleasure. I projected onto him that these were special relational times that he did not share with others. On these walks I started to notice this tall, red-haired, slender, fit man with his deep chocolate cocker spaniel in the dog park. As Jasper was my consistent accessory, this unknown man's cocker was by his side at all times. There was a dance, it seems, during this time in my life of going on so-so dates one night and seeing this man and his dog the next day. It took me a while to become curious as to what the universe might be suggesting, or about the direction that Jasper was taking me.

When I would arrive at the dog park, this man was often seated on a wooden bench, book opened on his lap, with his cocker's head draped over his right foot as the dog lay peacefully next to his sparkling green-eyed companion. There was something so sweet between them. They shared a joined space with comfort—one engrossed in a book and the other resting on his master's foot.

As my so-so dates went on, I kept seeing this man and his dog. Then, as if visiting a new land I started to see him other places in town, with and without his dog. "He is handsome," I thought, as if surprised. My intrigue only increased—not only was I drawn to his tender and engaged relationship with his dog (where I could project all sorts of admiring personality traits) but he was handsome.

One weekend day, lying on my sofa with Jasper curled up against my belly and C-shaped body, following another so-so date from the night before, I told myself with conviction that the next time I saw the man-with-dog, the handsome man, I would do the thing I had never done before—I would ask him out on a date. With power I don't possess, I saw this man through my ground floor condo window. Not giving myself the opportunity to let anxiety intrude and reverse the claim to myself, I grabbed Jasper, despite his startled and glazed look, tucked him under my right arm, and quickly made my way to the front door. I opened the door, and there was that man, without his dog, talking to a neighbor on my stoop. My female neighbor said, "Hi"—we had talked before, were fond of one another, and had shared our journeys to being single. The red-haired man said, "Hi." We all made idle chit-chat. Sensing our mutual attraction, the neighbor friend graciously reduced the math by one, "Oh, I forgot that I have to call my mother. Nice

to meet you (nodding to the tall red-haired one). Bradley, nice to see you." As she turned and walked away, this handsome man smiled. Oh my, he has a wonderful smile—one that brightens and lifts his face, as if generated from his sternum pushing upward.

I introduced myself. "Hi, I'm Bradley."

"I'm Bill." (He goes by William now and has for 10 years.)

"Nice to meet you, Bill. This is Jasper. I have seen you with your dog a bunch in the park."

"Yes, I have noticed. My dog's name is Roscoe." It was no longer the man with his dog, but Bill and Roscoe.

We chatted a bit. It was now or never. "Would you like to go out sometime and get a drink?" I wasn't sure why I said "get a drink"—I almost never drink. It's what you ask, I thought, shielding myself from my incoming shame. Just as I had that thought, Bill said, "I'd like that, but I don't drink." Though I had grabbed Jasper on my rush out the door, I had no paper or phone—remember I was a novice at this, a sort-of-but-not-really-40-year-old-virgin. "Sorry, I don't have a piece of paper or pen." "No problem," Bill said and pulled out a card with just his name and phone number on it. What is this? Cards for dates? I knew nothing of such readiness and smooth operating techniques.

I waited the customary 2 days that friends educated me about before I called Bill. We set up a date for the following weekend. In anticipation of our date, I kept holding the image of Bill in the park, book opened, and Roscoe draped over his foot. It brought a smile to my face and sternum. It still does.

We went to a local restaurant in Adam's Morgan, DC. The restaurant was in fact both of our favorite. We didn't have dinner. That was too much of a commitment. We had dessert. I don't remember what I had, but I do remember his green eyes that were still piercing despite it being nighttime.

We decided to take a walk through a local park. Historically, I didn't believe in magical moments. I was a realist. This felt enchanting.

The evening was coming to an end. I had something important to tell him. If he agreed to a second date, he had a right to know. "I'd like to go out again," I mustered up.

"I would as well."

"Good, but there is something I need to tell you." When a gay man says, "there is something I need to tell you," it often means he is HIV+. I didn't allow too much airtime to invite that fear to settle in before I said, "I'm pregnant."

Bill laughed—not a deep belly laugh but a restrained one that suited his elegance.

"No, really, sort of true. I'm in the very beginning stages of adopting a kid from Vietnam."

Bill paused for more time than I was comfortable with. Then he shifted his body weight towards one foot, tilted his head, and said, "Wow. I haven't thought about that for myself. Can you tell me how you came to that desire and decision at this time in your life?"

This is what was missing from all those so-so dates. Bill had claimed a truth about himself and was sincerely curious about me. He wanted to know my process of a long-standing desire to be a parent. I was so filled, delighted, and honestly, aroused, that I don't remember how I answered him. I do remember that after I answered he said, "I'm looking forward to our next date."

Roscoe lived until he was 14—about 7 years into our relationship. Roscoe was such a

sweet and loving soul. I can't write about him without tears covering the surface of my eyes.

Jasper lived until he was 19. To be honest though, Jasper adored me and I him, but he wasn't nearly as sweet as Roscoe.

When it was time to say good-bye to Roscoe I was by Bill's side. In our decades together I have rarely seen Bill cry, but he allowed himself the indulgence, in my presence, when Roscoe died. When it was time to say goodbye to Jasper, William was there (by then the transition from Bill to William had occurred). I have very few barriers to crying in front of others.

Since the passing of Roscoe and Jasper, we have loved, honored, and cared for four other dogs—and adopted two children, a boy and a girl. Daisy Mae was a spiritual, rescued, 85-lb German shorthaired pointer, who we lost way too young and quickly to cancer. Daisy Mae was to help our son Gabe with his profound anxiety with big dogs. From the first night we brought Daisy Mae home, Gabe and his companion slept in the same bed—every night. We still have Etta, a 12-lb Havanese. Etta was our daughter Ellie's transitional object to help her with the move out of DC to the Eastern Shore of Maryland. Etta and Ellie have a special and meaningful attachment. Etta is currently 9 1/2. And then there is Blueberry: a loving and now aging adopted beagle. Though no dog can replace Roscoe, Blue is William's dog. Blue sleeps snuggled up to William every moment she can. Blue had clearly been mistreated, and William's dog-whispering ways have brought the true spirit of loving warmth to the forefront in her nature. We think Blue is probably around 11 or 12 now. Libby, our latest, is a 75-lb Bernedoodle from a ranch in Colorado. She was born on the Fourth of July, 2017. Libby is short for Liberty.

She is the family's dog, spreading her love to all of us, but when given the chance she is deeply attached to me, and I feel it. I feel it in my soul. I feel it when she's on the sofa with her big hairy face resting on my lap. I feel it when she looks directly into my eyes—eyes locked—in the way lovers do. I feel it as she sleeps on top of me every night. I love Libby, and she loves me.

Etta, Blue, and Libby sleep in William's and my bed every night. If it wasn't for seeing the red-haired man with his chocolate cocker, their bond and relational ways, and my courage to enter the new territory of asking someone out, this menagerie—this collective, robust, wild, crazy, and love-filled family of two kids and three dogs—would have never happened.

Roscoe, I miss you terribly. Jasper, thank you for your companionship and choosing to love me. Roscoe and Jasper, I am grateful to both of your spirited selves for guiding William and me into this journey together. William, I am blessed to love and be married to a dog whisperer, even if you think my love for dogs is over the top.

"Hon, can we get a 4th dog."

"NO!"

Every engine needs a brake.

Me and God One Morning

Tom Large

No need for a monument here
in my small yard, not edged
and hosting lots of dandelions.
Nothing for TV news to film
up and down my street,
where the only action this morning
has been the walking of dogs
and prodding children off to school.
Doing yard work I see no reason
to gussy up the ordinary,
watering the rhododendron that looks dry
or weeding around these roses.
I'm here alone and puttering,
relatively conscious, thinking we need rain,
thinking this laurel should be trimmed
for a moment caught in the wonder of just being.
Everything is fallen into place.
I am the same borrowed dust
as this lowly grass and shrubbery,
the same stuff as these taxi-colored bees
stopping on the azalea blooms
and paying no attention
to the urgent fuss I make
going to write this down.
It's as if the day itself,
like my grandmother when she came to visit,
has gathered me up in her arms.

Stephanie Ezust, PhD

Decatur, Georgia
drezust@comcast.net

Book Review

The Book of Hope: A Survival Guide for Trying Times
by Jane Goodall and Douglas Abrams, with Gail Hudson,
Celadon Books,
New York, NY
2021, 272 pages

The timing of this book's publication was probably intentional, as a ray of light coming out of what seems like a time of universal darkness. This is a book I want to buy for everyone I care about. The format is a conversation between Douglas Abrams and Jane Goodall, which some people might find a bit unwieldy, but I enjoyed the informality and the growing intimacy between them. Abrams had previously published a conversation with Desmond Tutu and the Dalai Lama, *The Book of Joy*, the first in the Global Icons Series (Dalai Lama et al., 2016). The Goodall book is the second in that series. Jane Goodall, now aged 88, is billed on the flap as "the world's most famous living naturalist." As her story unfolds through their conversations, her courage and her spirit are gently portrayed.

Goodall began her journey as a naturalist working with Louis Leakey in Kenya in 1957. She was one of the "trimates" mentored by Leakey (Dian Fossey, who worked with mountain gorillas, and Birutė Galdikas, who worked with orangutans, were the other two). She spent many months in the bush observing the chimps there, eventually, like the Little Prince and the fox (Saint-Exupery, 1943), connecting with them. And there is something about the metaphor of taming the fox, as Goodall patiently tamed the chimps, that parallels our work as therapists.

Goodall lists four reasons for holding hope for the world, expanding on each: (a) what she calls the amazing human intellect, (b) the resilience of nature, (c) the power of young people, and (d) the indomitable human spirit.

I did not realize that there is a growing field of hope science. The reference section at the end of the book provides information about current research, among many other resources. Hope, according to Goodall, does not deny that there is evil in the world but is a response to it, which is not to be confused with idealism. Hope takes facts and obstacles into account but doesn't let them overwhelm or stop us.

In discussing what she calls the amazing human intellect, Goodall distinguishes between intellectual and intelligent, pointing out that an intelligent animal would not destroy its only home. That said, she talks about the qualities that humans possess that allow for the hope she holds: the mastery of language, which has allowed humans to pass on knowledge about things that are not present, so that we can pass on wisdom from experience and plan for the distant future, as well as being able to explore issues and problems (not always used to greatest benefit by all humans, but this is not a political review!). She notes that language, goal setting, and hope all originate in the prefrontal cortex. She observes that while only humans are capable of true evil, such that we can sit down and cold-bloodedly work out ways to torture and inflict pain, we are also the only creatures capable of true altruism. Abrams cites Desmond Tutu, who said that forgiveness is how we unchain ourselves from the past, that we can choose the forgiveness cycle rather than the revenge cycle, as evidenced by the Reconciliation Process in South Africa following the end of Apartheid.

Goodall observes that in order to use this amazing human intellect wisely, we must solve four great challenges: (a) alleviate poverty, (b) reduce the unsustainable lifestyles of the affluent, (c) eliminate corruption, and (d) deal with the population growth of humans and their livestock.

Her second reason for hope is the resilience of nature. They reference a report from the American Psychological Association that concludes that climate crises can cause people to experience a whole range of feelings including helplessness, depression, fear, fatalism, resignation, and eco-grief or eco-anxiety. In order to overcome the despair and powerlessness that so easily render us stuck, it is important to face our grief about climate change, a dynamic that we as psychotherapists know well when we encounter denial in our clients. I think that the core of her message of hope is that the cumulative effect of small ethical actions will truly make a difference. And when we work with clients to develop resilience, we find that adaptability is an important component. This is true regarding our response to climate change and is perhaps the greatest obstacle facing climate change deniers. Goodall notes the link between nature's resilience and human resilience. Addressing human injustices such as poverty and gender oppression creates hope for people and the environment as well. Protecting endangered species preserves biodiversity on the Earth, and as we protect all life, we protect our own.

The third reason for hope is the power of young people. Goodall reminds Abrams of a famous saying, "We have not inherited the Earth from our ancestors, but borrowed it from our children," but she laments that we have not borrowed it; we have stolen it! I think part of Goodall's legacy will be her establishment of the Roots & Shoots programs, which have now sprouted all over the world. As of the printing of the book, there were hundreds of thousands of members, from kindergarten through university, active in 68 countries. These are groups of young people who have begun programs within their own communities, often in some of the seemingly most hopeless places on the planet. For example, the Pine Ridge Reservation in North Dakota had one of the highest suicide rates in the United States, with three to six attempts a week. The Native Americans, who had once been the guardians of the earth, had now, for the most part, lost that connection. So starting these grass roots programs, where the children began to reconnect with the land, was transformative. On the Pine Ridge Reservation, the Roots & Shoots group has begun using the Hidatsa method for growing crops, in which the planting of the "three sisters" of corn, beans, and squash together produces high quality yields with minimal environmental impact. The corn provides the support for the beans to climb; the beans replenish nutrients in the soil; and the large squash leaves provide living mulch and shade, conserve water, and control weeds—a beautiful metaphor for cooperative living.

Another Roots & Shoots program began in Burundi, a country that many of us may not know about. As I read this description, I found myself feeling some shame that I knew nothing about Burundi. It is just south of Rwanda, and while the genocidal war that took place in Rwanda received much publicity, which generated support, healing, and hope, Burundi got no attention for the atrocities going on there. As a result, this country has not recovered in the way that Rwanda has. A young Congolese man started a Roots & Shoots program there, after his entire family was massacred in Congo. The program spread throughout Burundi and has been transformative: One boy told Goodall, "My village was like a desert, but now trees are found everywhere, and the rain comes regularly" (p. 140). Other children told her that there are no more forest fires, the air is fresh, and the animals have returned to the forest, because the hunting has stopped.

Abrams asked Goodall if she had met Greta Thunberg, who famously told the World Economic Forum:

> Adults keep saying 'We owe it to young people to give them hope.' But I don't want your hope. I don't want you to be hopeful. I want you to panic. I want you to feel the fear I feel every day, and then I want you to act. I want you to act as you would in a crisis. I want you to act as if our house is on fire, because it is. (p. 127)

Goodall's response:

> We *do* need to respond with fear and anger about what is happening. Our house *is* on fire. But if we don't have hope that we can put the fire out, we will give up. It's not hope *or* fear—*or* anger. We need them all. (p. 127)

The fourth reason for hope is what Goodall calls the indomitable human spirit. She says that our ability to deliberately tackle what seems impossible and not give up, even though we know we may not succeed or that it may kill us, is an important aspect of this spirit and that it requires imagination, determination, resilience, and courage. Abrams again invokes Tutu: Suffering can either embitter us or ennoble us, and it tends to ennoble us if we are able to make meaning out of our suffering and use it for the benefit of others. This evokes Victor Frankl's (1959) wonderful memoir of his experience in Auschwitz, *Man's Search for Meaning*. They both agree that having a sense of humor is also important. Abrams related that his son had suffered a traumatic brain injury and that as part of his healing he began doing stand-up comedy. Goodall commented that in order to foster resiliency in children, they need consistent nurturing, safety, and care. As a clinician working with trauma survivors, I know that research has shown that those adults traumatized as children who had at least one positive relationship with an adult had the best chance of developing coping strategies to help them heal.

An important takeaway from *Hope* is that we cannot continue to live on our planet as we have. One of the great threats is our dependence on eating animals, and one of the solutions is to cultivate a plant-based diet. In addition, one of the effects of overpopulation is the encroachment on the habitats of wildlife. And as we crowd out wildlife, we also invite disease. The dialogue between Abrams and Goodall was interrupted by the lockdown caused by the pandemic and had to be concluded virtually. In the concluding chapter, Goodall says:

> We must not let this [the pandemic] distract us from the greater threat to our future—the climate crisis and the loss of biodiversity—for if we cannot solve these threats, then it will be the end of life on Earth as we know it, including our own. We cannot live on if the natural world dies. (p. 231-232)

Years ago, a clinical supervisor taught me an idea to present to clients who were consumed with depression and hopelessness, a message that this book epitomizes. She taught me to tell my clients that I would hold their hope until they were ready to reclaim it. And although I have found this hope a slippery entity to hold on to, I have been able to grasp it sufficiently to offer to my clients during this dark time. This book is a manual for holding on to hope. ▼

References

Dalai Lama [Gyatso, T.], Tutu, D., & Abrams, D. (2016). *The book of joy: Lasting happiness in a changing world.* New York: Avery.

Frankl, V. (1959). *Man's search for meaning.* Boston, MA: Beacon Press.

Saint-Exupery, A. (1943). *The little prince.* New York: Reynal & Hitchcock.

> Hope is often misunderstood. People tend to think it is simply passive wishful thinking: I hope something will happen but I'm not going to do anything about it. This is indeed the opposite of real hope, which requires action and engagement.
>
> —Jane Goodall, p. xiii-xiv

> Hope is an innate survival trait that seems to exist in every child's head and heart; but even so, it needs to be encouraged and cultivated. If it is, hope can take root, even in the grimmest of situations...
>
> —Jane Goodall, p. 138

Impasse, Intrigue, & Inspiration: Effecting Change through Psychotherapy

Winter 2022

Call for Papers

Deadline for submission: August 15, 2022

Direct questions and submissions to the editor, Carla Bauer, LCSW *crbauer01@bellsouth.net*

See Submission Guidelines on the AAP website: **www.aapweb.com** or in any issue of *Voices*

PEOPLE COME TO THERAPY TO CHANGE—OR DO THEY?—YET CLIENTS OFTEN RESIST THAT VERY CHANGE.

Ever feel stuck when working with a client? The therapy seems stalled, at an impasse—now what? Perhaps your steady client has hit a plateau and can't seem to move forward. What about that ambivalent one who never quite seems fully invested, or the frustrated client with one foot out the door? How do you motivate that resistant patient who just won't do anything different to change what isn't working in her life? How do you break the impasse and motivate change?

Are you intrigued about the topics your clients talk about—and don't talk about!—wondering why they're paying to talk about that? Are you left wondering just what keeps them coming? What about those surprises when your patient buries the lead or drops a major revelation while walking out the door?

For this issue of Voices, consider: What have been some of your most challenging moments in psychotherapy? When have you felt stymied, not sure what to do next? When have you been caught off guard by something your client said—whether a door knob moment or an unexpected revelation that changed your formulation of the case? What about those moments when you hear, too late, how your words landed on your client's ears with a heavy thud, threatening a conflictual impasse? What inspired breakthrough in such scenarios? What have been your successes and struggles in motivating change? What would you do differently, given a do-over?

Consider: how do such moments of impasse impact your sense of self as therapist, your confidence in your abilities or impact? Consider, too, when you have felt stuck in your own life. How have you broken your own impasses and ambivalence for the change you sought, heeded (or not) your own therapeutic advice, to unstick your own life? How has your own experience informed your work with clients?

Also for consideration: While not specifically a pandemic theme, perhaps this surreal time has brought its own impasses and/or previously unattainable resolutions to former ones?

Voices welcomes submissions in the form of personal essay, research- and case-based inquiry, poetry, art, cartoons and photography.

The American Academy of Psychotherapists invites you to be a part of an enlightening journey into...

VOICES

Voices is a uniquely rewarding publication providing a meeting ground with other experienced psychotherapists. A theme-oriented journal, *Voices* presents personal and experiential essays by therapists from a wide range of orientations. Each issue takes you on an intimate journey through the reflections of therapists as they share their day-to-day experiences in the process of therapy. *Voices'* contributors reveal insights inherent in our lives, our culture and our society.

As a subscriber, you'll have the opportunity to experience contributions from noted luminaries in psychotherapy. Using various styles from articles to poems, *Voices* is interdisciplinary in its focus, reflecting the aims and mission of its publisher, the American Academy of Psychotherapists.

VOICES SUBSCRIPTION

Please start my one-year subscription to AAP's journal *Voices* at $65 for individuals PDF only; $85 for individuals PDF & print copy. Institutional subscriptions may be reserved directly through the AAP office or through the traditional subscription agencies at $249 per year. *Voices* is published electronically three times per year and is delivered to your email address as an ePublication.

Name ....

Address ....

City .... State .... ZIP ....

Telephone .... Fax ....

Email ....

❑ My check made payable to AAP *Voices* is enclosed.

❑ Please charge to my credit card, using the information I have supplied below:

Form of payment: ❑ Master Card ❑ Visa

Account # .... Expiration: ....

Signature ....

Address all orders by mail to:

Voices
230 Washington Ave Ext, Suite 101
Albany, NY 12203
You may also fax your order to (518) 240-1178.
For further information, please call (518) 694-5360

Made in the USA
Columbia, SC
22 May 2022

60764027R00057